THE LITTLE BREADWINNER

*"There is no crown more worthy
than a child breadwinner."*

THE LITTLE BREADWINNER

A STORY OF WAR AND SURVIVAL

- INSPIRED BY TRUE EVENTS -

LUCIA MANN

■:■ Aperion Books

AGOURA HILLS, CALIFORNIA

Aperion Books™

AGOURA HILLS, CALIFORNIA

10 9 8 7 6 5 4 3 2
First Edition 2020

Printed in the United States of America

ISBN: 978-0-9856039-3-9
Library of Congress Control Number: 2020916422

Cover & book design by CenterPointe Media
www.CenterPointeMedia.com

Dedication

I would like to dedicate this book to the thousands
of innocent souls who were stripped of all human
rights and who lost their lives by the National
Guard, military death squads, during
the "dirty" El Salvadoran Civil War,
aided by the U.S. government.

Author's Note

To help readers understand and follow this story, I've appended a map and historical chronology that shaped this Latin American country before and after the full-fledged civil war took place between 1980 and 1992.

Acknowledgements

I am genuinely thankful to all those who have once more supported me on this seventh book-writing journey. Thank you, Terrin Erwin, for the finest proofing. Thank you, Matthew, for being by my side yet again on our onward journey.

Thank you to friends who displayed my books in their stores: Trish Albertine (Brewing on Broadway). Larry Ferguson (Home Hardware) and Heather Maxfield (Treasure Trove).

Thank you, Simon Wallis and Pam Isbell for your support and encouragement. To all my ardent readers—virtual hugs. And to Deb Booth who did my photos and transformed an extinct Dodo into a princess!

More than fifty years ago, I vowed I would not stop being the "voice" of victims of wrongdoings in my writings. I intend to keep this pledge for as long as there is breath in my aging body.

El Salvador Map

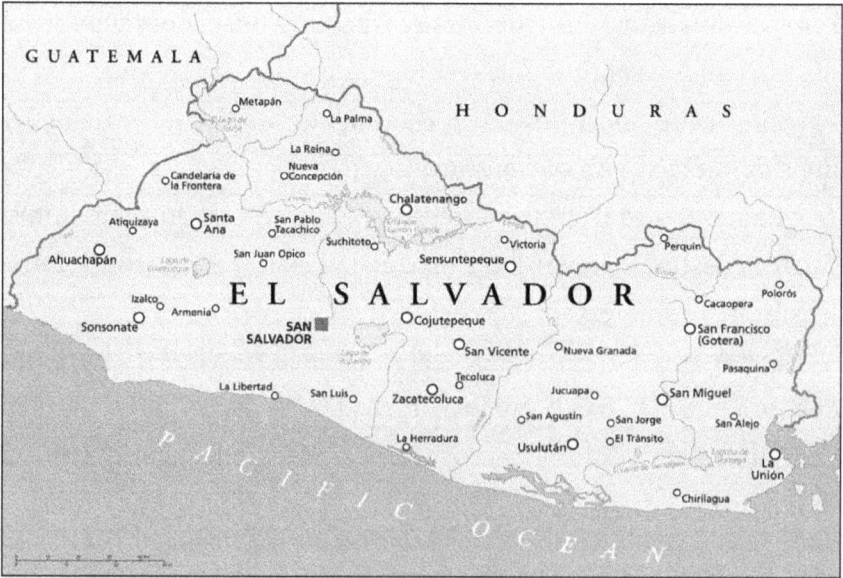

Table of Contents

Chronology of Key Events That Shaped the Central American Country of El Salvador
- BASED ON HISTORICAL FACTS -

1524   Spanish adventurer Pedro de Alvarado conquers El Salvador.

1540   Indigenous resistance finally crushed, and El Salvador becomes a Spanish colony.

1821   El Salvador gains independence from Spain. Conflict ensues over the territory's incorporation into the Mexican Empire under Creole general Agustin de Iturbide.

1840   El Salvador becomes fully independent following the United Provinces of Central America.

1859   President Gerardo Barrios introduces coffee growing.

1932   30,000 people died during the suppression of a peasant uprising led by Agustine Farabundo Marti.

1961   Ring-wing National Conciliation Party (PCN) comes to power after a military coup.

1969   El Salvador attacks and fights a brief war with neighboring Honduras following the eviction of thousands of Salvadoran illegal immigrants from Honduras.

1977   Guerrilla activities by the left-wing Farabundo Marti National Liberation Front intensify amid reports of increased human rights violations by government troops and death squads. General Carlos Romero elected president.

1979   Army-backed death squads slaughter thousands of people.

1980   El Salvador's civil war officially began.

1980   Archbishop of San Salvador and human rights campaigner Óscar Romero assassinated; Jose Napoleon Duarte becomes the first civilian president.

Civilians resign from the national government.

FMLN formed.

Death threats and two bombs received at the University of Central America.

Ronald Reagan elected US president.

Six FMLN leaders kidnapped and killed by the El Salvadoran military.

Four US church workers abducted, raped, and killed.

1981   France and Mexico recognize the FMLN as legitimate political force; US continues to assist El Salvadoran government whose army backs right-wing death squads.

FMLN began military attacks.

Salvadoran military took over the University of Central America.

During US President Carter's presidency 5 million dollars aided the Salvadoran military.

1982 President Reagan approved human rights standards in El Salvador.

1983 President Reagan asked Congress to send more aid to El Salvador.

1984 Napolean Duarte (Christian Democrat) wins the presidential election.

Five National Guard members are convicted in the murders of church women.

Peace talks began.

US Kissinger Commission called for more aid and examination of human rights issues.

1985 FMLN kidnapped Duarte's daughter and her friend.

Father Ellacuria and Monsignor Riveras Damas negated the girls' release.

1986 Duarte begins the quest for a negotiated settlement with FMLN.

Peace talks fell apart.

ARENA party increased power.

1987 Peace talks began again.

The US increased aid to El Salvador.

1988 Father Ellacuria met with FMLN leaders in Nicaragua.

Father Ellacuria and Father Montes (Catholic leaders in El Salvador) met with future Salvadoran president, Alfredo Cristiani.

President Bush elected US president.

1989 February, US Vice President Dan Quayle visited El Salvador and warned against further human rights violations.

Alfredo Cristiani became Salvadoran president.

April, the Salvadoran Attorney General Roberto Garcia Alvarado is murdered.

June, the Minister of Presidency, Jose Antonio Rodriguez Porth, is murdered.

October, the daughter of Colonel Eduardo Casanova Vejar of the Salvadoran military is assassinated.

November, the US Assistant Secretary of State, Bernard Aronson, calls for Peace.

National Trade Union Federation bombed.

President Cristiani asked Father Ellacuria (Catholic Leader of El Salvador) to help investigate the bombing.

FMLN attacked military centers in major cities.

Military bombed residential neighborhoods believed to support the FMLN.

US pulled-out non-essential military personnel.

November 15, secret meeting held to plan the assassination of Father Ellacuria.

November 16, six priests, their housekeeper, and her daughter are murdered at UCA.

December, Congressman Joe Moakley led the Speaker's Salvadoran investigation.

FMLN attacks intensify; another Arena candidate, Álvaro Cristiani, voted president in elections widely believed to have been rigged.

1990   Colonel Benavidas of the Salvadoran military arrested for November 16 murders.

February, Congressman Moakley visited El Salvador.

April, Congressman Moakley filled his official report.

UN became involved. Serious peace talks finally began.

US House of Representatives voted for a 50% decrease in aid to El Salvador.

1991   FMLN recognized as political party; government and FMLN sign UN-sponsored peace accord.

FMLN killed two U.S. military advisors.

Congressman Moakley reported that the El Salvadoran military is controlling investigations.

Congress increased aid to El Salvador by 50%.

Colonel Benavides and Lieutenant Mendoza convicted in November of the murders at UCA.

Moakley reported that high military officials planned the murders.

Military and FMLN signed a peace agreement in New York.

1992   Peace Accords of El Salvador signed in Mexico.

Cease-fire began under UN supervision.

UN Truth Commission began an investigation of human rights violations.

UN Secretary-General found the El Salvadoran military, not in compliance with the peace accords.

UN released findings from investigations.

Top military officials resign in El Salvador

1993   The government declares amnesty for those implicated by UN-sponsored commission in human rights atrocities.

1994   Elections held in El Salvador. ARENA party wins, candidate Armando Calderon Sol elected president. FMLN comes in second.

1996　Second elections, FMLN wins 45% of the National Assembly and mayor of San Salvador.

1999　Lawsuit against Generals Garcia and Casanova of the Salvadoran military for the 1980 church-workers' murders begin.

2000　The US constructed a military base at the Salvadoran national airport.

The court found Generals Garcia and Casanova not responsible for murders.

Salvadoran Attorney General began an investigation against the former president, Cristiani, and other top officials.

2002　Generals Garcia and Casanova found guilty for allowing their men to kidnap, torture, rape, and murder thousands of unarmed civilians.

Introduction

El Salvador ("The Savior") Central America

(Named by the Spanish conquerors in 1524)

Was the United States justified in providing billions of dollars in aid to the El Salvadoran military during the Civil War?

In the aftermath of the slaughter of civilians, who "conveniently" stole confidential files containing the "proof" of these heinous violations?

Did the CIA interfere? Were "they" responsible for stealing the files, containing evidence in the survivors' testimonies?

Undoubtedly!

El Salvador is a small Central (8,000sq.miles) American

country that is bordered by Honduras, Guatemala, and the Pacific Ocean. Equivalent to 0.08% of the total world population, El Salvador is known to have been beleaguered by violence and overwhelming crushing poverty due to the over-population and class struggles in which most Salvadoran citizens were affected. (The conflict between rich and poor of this named third-world country has existed for centuries, and continues to present day.)

In the 1880s, coffee became a major cash crop for El Salvador. It brought in 95% of the country's income. However, this new-found prosperity became confined within only 2% of the population. As the rich grew more prosperous, the poor became more deprived of basic living, and tensions between the upper and lower classes worsened, paving the way for rebellion—the communist ideology of "fairness"— in times to come.

By the 1900s, El Salvador's continuing unrest became "ripe" for a proletarian-like man, a Marxist-Leninist activist named Agustín Farabundo Martí (1893-1932). This budding liberal reformist was born in Teotepeque, a small rural farming community located in Departamento de La Libertad. (Agustín's father, a moderate landowner, reputedly adopted his last name in honor of the Cuban patriot José Martí.)

Young Agustín Martí grew up surrounded by *campesinos* (peasants), with whom he identified later in life. After graduating from the "Salesian Secondary School," the bright scholar enrolled in the University of El Salvador to study social and political sciences. Right from the beginning of his academic studies, Martí became exasperated by the lack of open discussion by faculty members and other leftist students. So he took it upon himself to independently read anarchist and communist texts in the university's library. The bright scholar formed beliefs that the exploration of his country's poor people was for the profit of the rich who grew wealthier by the day.

Greed-economics didn't sit well with the fired-up Agustín Martí.

The restless student dropped out of university and turned his focus to the emerging labor movement. He began alluring the poor and the underprivileged with disgruntled hearts into a rebellion against the Melédez-Quiñoez dynasty, who was ruling the country at this time. Martí's primary aspiration was to fight for his community and nation and eventually partook in the first-ever strikes held in El Salvador in 1920. The fanatical young man held secret underground meetings to rally the *campesinos* along with the country's indigenous people to rise against the Salvadoran government. It would be a tragic decision.

In retaliation to this uprising, the government-supported military death-squads shot peasants along with anyone who even looked Indian or who could be helping Martí's insurgency. The killings became known as "*La Matanza*" (The Massacre), in which 30,000 people perished.

In the wake of this heinous massacre, Agustín and his comrade, José Luis Barrientos, was arrested. Four days later, the comrades were released from prison and exiled from El Salvador. This political strategy was to retain civil order because the last thing the government wanted was: a further uprising if the execution of these traitors was carried out. In government mindsets, their deaths would simply make them martyrs.

(Without documented proof of this claim, Martí and Barrientos supposedly spent their banishment living among the isolated Quiché Maya Indians to evade assassination by hired government shooters to hunt them down.)

⚭

By December of 1925, Agustín found a way to reenter El Salvador once more. He took refuge on a rural farm not far from where he was born. From his hide-out, the ardent leftist continued where he had left off, raising the class-consciousness of the poor agricultural workers. His followers revered him. Agustín's popularity did not go undetected by those now in power.

Upon receiving intelligence briefings regarding the anarchist's continuing revolution, President Alfonso Molina immediately had Agustín rearrested. Following his capture, he spent the closing years of the 1920s in an El Salvadoran penitentiary, with intermittent periods of exile.

However, this shrewd-minded revolutionist was well underestimated by political leaders.

⚭

Once more, Martí secretly made his way back into El Salvador just in time for the December 1930 election campaign in which the Salvadoran Communists refused to participate. Instead, the leftists now concentrated their efforts on organizing the dispossessed rural peasantry. Agustín planned *another* mass uprising, but to his chagrin, the government uncovered the plot.

He, along with two student accomplices, were executed by firing squad in late 1932. Eight years after their deaths, the civil war began, initiated by the military-led junta government and the Farbunda Martí National Liberation Front, FMLN—a coalition, also known as the "umbrella organization" in honor of their model Agustín Martí—from October 15, 1979, to January 16, 1992.

⟳

DOCUMENTED FACTS

An unknown number of individuals disappeared during this U.S. funded conflict.

Cuban-backed guerrillas were held only accountable for 5% of the murders during this brutal civil war, while the Salvadoran military death squads executed 85% from 1980 to 1992, and were not held accountable for their unethical acts. The brainwashed killers' wiped-out entire villages believed to be in cahoots with, the guerrilla efforts. This genocidal conflict killed an estimated 75,000 El Salvadoran civilians, mostly poor peasants and indigenous people. However, it wasn't just the lower classes, singled out for death. The premeditated murders of social hierarchy included unionists, clergy, independent farmers, university officials, and the highly revered Archbishop Óscar Romero, who was shot to death by a sniper while conducting Mass. Following the archbishop's death were also four American churchwomen, six Jesuit priests, their housekeeper, and her raped daughter were also shot to death. These guiltless souls died at the hands of the government forces. Even a government is capable of the lowest of acts!

Prologue

Los Indios, Mexico

- MONDAY, AUGUST 12, 2019 -

"We're born afraid; we're all afraid of things: death, disfigurement, loss of a loved one."
—JOHN CARPENTER

The twenty-eight-year-old with subnormal development, the mind of a child, squealed aloud, "Where are you, Mamacita (Little Mother)?"

Her nose was running from tears building up her nasal passages. The mentally-challenged female addressed her mother's absence with concerned internal dialogue: *You told me you were going to the store to buy milk, and you didn't come back! Please come home now! I'm hungry and frightened.*

Named after the slain Archbishop Óscar Romero's deceased infant sister, Aminta slithered out of her wheelchair onto the floor, and then glided her deformed limbs beneath the bed she shared with her mother. Disfigured hands reached upwards for a blanket to wrap around her trembling body. There, in her dark haven, Aminta wept while sucking her thumb.

After what seemed to be an eternity, the fretful young woman slunk from her hiding place and maneuvered her disabled body onto the mobility chair. The crackling of wheels over a plywood subfloor headed for the kitchen area. Aminta leaned forward, and with teeth clenched, tugged at the string tied to the refrigerator handle that her mother had designed for her to have easy access. Aminta's features contorted with disgust. The slim pickings on the shelves would never satisfy a hungry, growling stomach: one yellow-skinned banana with lots of brown spots, one wrinkled orange, a small piece of molding cheese, and a can of lemon soda.

A misshapen hand slammed the refrigerator door shut. Aminta then wheeled herself to a cupboard across the room. Large brown eyes scanned the food shelf: a small bag of rice, a coffee tin, and one small packet of dried frijole beans. Overpowered by a distraught demeanor, she bellowed, "Mamacita, come home *NOW!*"

Incensed tears falling, Aminta returned to her haven under the bed. Another day passed. The outlook was bleak.

In acute crisis mode, Aminta stared warily out the bedroom window, whimpering pitifully, "Mamacita, I will *die* if you don't come home." Where *was* Estrella (Moon Star) Lozano Fuentes—Mamacita? It would remain unanswered for now.

Chapter One

Laredo, Texas

- THE NEXT DAY, TUESDAY, AUGUST 13, 2019 -

"Thou shalt not be a victim, thou shalt not be a perpetrator, but, above all, thou shalt not be a bystander."
—Yehuda Bauer

In this hottest month, a crimson-red sun dipped below the horizon, heading to its resting place. As evening approached, breathless shadows began to cast mirage shapes over the semiarid landscape. Later, streetlights would shimmer in the background throughout the city. Laredo, bordering Nuevo Laredo in the state of Tamaulipas, Mexico, is a notorious territory of drug trafficking by ruthless Mexican cartels.

On this night at 11.25 p.m., U.S. Border Patrol agents Dwayne Carlton Dalton and Cesar Luis Rivas reported for duty—the graveyard shift. After signing in, the uniformed men in lightweight jackets tight over bodybuilders' chests left the station headquarters, heading for a vehicle parked in the fenced lot.

Behind the wheel of a 4x4 government-registered truck, Agent Dalton drove down backroads to begin the often dangerous work, patrolling along the northern banks of the Rio Grande River. The partners' exchanged light conversation as to how their day had gone, then Dwayne remarked, "I wonder what *this* night brings us?"

"Who knows," was Cesar's casual reply as he reached into his backpack to retrieve his night vision scope, essential for detecting *crossers* such as drug smugglers, called mules, coyotes, or *polleros* who help people flee from Latin American countries. The agents were long cognizant of the human traffickers who charged large sums of money for bringing *clients*: whole families, men and women, boys, and girls, as young as thirteen, and even pregnant women into the U.S. illegally. The money-hungry "coyotes" earn their living from desperate people, generally under the cloak of night. However, their means of illicit transport are rendered useless when discovered by the border guards as they attempt the crossing of the Río Grande.

The Rio Grande is the fifth longest river in North America. From its headwaters in the San Juan Mountains of Southwestern Colorado, this mighty fabled river flows through the state of Texas and the Mexican states of Chihuahua, Coahuila, Nuevo Leon, and Tamaulipas, into the Gulf of Mexico. It is a recognized river of tragedy, bringing death, injury, and human desperation.

⚭

On this moonless, windless night, shortly after midnight

Dwayne Dalton removed his cowboy hat and ran his fingers through a mop of ginger hair that matched his fiery temper. "Time to get to work," he stated, raising his night vision scope to eye-level. Through infrared thermal imaging Dwayne spotted the bundle upriver on the U.S. border side of the Rio Grande. "It looks like we have a "drop," he commented aloud.

It wasn't unusual for abandoned drugs to be beached along the shores by "spooked" drug traffickers evading capture. It wasn't unusual either for bundles of discarded clothing to wash up. Nevertheless, something niggled at Dwayne's trained-spotter mind. He once more raised his scope to eye level.

Powerful lenses now pinpointed what appeared to be a body lying face down in the murky waters. Dwayne's voice raised an octave, "Get over here *now!*" he instructed his partner, who was taking a bathroom break behind brambles.

"*Bien*…Okay, I'm coming," Cesar answered, hurriedly zipping up his Wranglers.

At his partner's side, Cesar queried, "What we got?"

"I think we have a *floater!*" Adrenalin kicked in.

The men waded through waters, carefully navigating the swirling currents to reach the mysterious object. For some unknown reason, a sense of unease surged through Cesar's Latino veins. His gut feeling was not unfounded because his powerful flashlight revealed the small form of a human body. Cesar swallowed hard before voicing, "Oh God, not another kid!"

"Great start to our shift," Dwayne muttered.

Wasting no time, the agents got to work, pulling out the face-down, fetal-positioned little body from its reedy entanglement.

Loud gasps of disbelief struck the humid air. Cesar's stunned reaction was, "Mother of God, it is a..."

"No, shit!" Dwayne interrupted.

The seasoned senior officers of more than twenty-five years' experience apiece thought they had seen all the stark realities of border life, until now. Part of their night-to-day function was to apprehend illegals, fish out bodies, and collect abandoned contraband bundles from the flowing waters. After all, their sworn duty was to guard the borders of the United States. However, it was evident that the influx of illegal crossers had surged in past months, dragged under by the violent currents while attempting to swim across this dangerous portal into the United States. In this year alone, hundreds of people fleeing from poverty, violence, wars, and misery, just seeking a better future, were recovered lifeless from the treacherous waters that separated Mexico from the United States. One tragedy in particular: the image of a father and daughter face down in the Rio Grande that shocked the world.

Óscar Alberto Martinez and his infant twenty-three-month-old daughter, Angie Valeria, natives of El Salvador, drowned trying to cross the dangerous river. The image of a little arm wrapped around her father's neck was a grim reminder of human desperation.

What had motivated their dangerous journey?

"They wanted to have their own home," Óscar's grieving mother stated to a reporter. "Anything better than the migrant holding in Matamoros, Mexico, (asylum camp), in conditions of hunger and overcrowding and in temperatures which soared over 110 degrees."

＊

In the days following this gut-wrenching tragedy, Dwayne and Cesar admitted to each other that they'd spent sleepless nights after watching the removal of the dead father and daughter from their watery graves on television.

That memory was still fresh in their minds on *this* night. What the veteran men were about to discover early on this Tuesday morning would overwhelm their psyches and spur endless night terrors for years.

Chapter Two

The Rio Grande

- IN THE SOMBER HOURS OF A NEW DAY -

"I will not let you go into the unknown alone."
—Abraham "Bram" Stoker

At first, there was grave-yard silence as the agents gaped at the naked little body. The eerie silence was punctuated by a loud exclamation from Dwayne, "Holy crap, this is a first!"

Cesar Rivas shut his eyelids tight as if to block out the disturbing sight. It was evident that this wasn't a drowning, but instead a violent homicide.

The dead female's chubby hands were tied behind her back, clearly indicating that she had not attempted to cross the river of her own free will. Most troubling was the fact that she had over fifty stab wounds and notable blunt force trauma to her head. The stunned agents were acutely aware of the death mortality by drowning, but this horrific murder of a *little person* was a *first*.

Cesar had seen numerous deaths by drowning that had occurred while on his watch, but the semblance of *this* fatality would burn in his memory forever. It would abide by a tragic personal memory that he didn't wish to revisit at this moment.

Staring downward at the mutilated body, the agents could still only speculate. In stunned silence, their prying minds individually swirled with looks that asked:

Who would do that to her?

It had to have been carried out by a cold and calculating killer, in a fit of evil rage!

Why?

Where was this sadistic perpetrator?

What was the motive?

Where was the murder weapon?

When did it happen?

How long had the body been in the water?

Was she murdered here, in Mexico, or elsewhere and then dumped in the river?

With internal questions pushed aside, Cesar jumped into action, retrieved his cellphone from his shirt pocket, and pressed SPEED-DIAL. "Dispatch, this is Senior Patrol Agent Cesar Luis Rivas. We have a homicide. The victim is a Hispanic adult female dwarf about four feet tall, and an estimated weight of 120 lbs. She's naked, her arms are tied behind her back with sisal rope, and she has multiple stab wounds and signs of excessive trauma all over her body..." His voice faltered for a few seconds before adding. "It appears blunt force trauma has caved in the right side of her skull." He didn't report the visible circular wounds on the victim's eyelids, nose, and mouth, which he knew was consistent with crabs or small fish nibbling on flesh. The senior of the agents continued to dispatch, "There are no defense wounds on her hands."

"Okay, we are on our way," said the voice at the other end of the line.

Hands clawed at pants legs as Cesar looked down at the deceased's matted, waterlogged gray hair; then he quietly deliberated: *How could someone do this to another person? It's the embodiment of evil. What the heck did this "little person" do to warrant this vicious murder?*

As if reading his partner's mind, Dwayne stated, "She had no chance against this kind of evil. I'd like to get my hands on the bastard who did this," he ended snarly.

"I wonder what was going through her mind on the last day of her life?" the tender-hearted Cesar remarked. "What terror did she encounter? I hope she was already dead when she hit the water!"

With numerous external and internal questions that had no immediate answers dangling in mid-air, Dwayne donned his cowboy hat, a silent indicator to his partner that it was "back to work buddy"—until the authorities show up. Cesar caught the drift, but he had something to do before going back to work. "I'll catch up with you," he said, "I would like to say a prayer for this poor woman."

Not being of any practicing faith, Dwayne replied, "Go ahead. I'm heading east to the inlet. See you there."

Cesar removed his cap and then plumped down on his haunches. With blurry moist eyes and unrequited sadness, he supplicated, "O God, I pray for this brutally murdered woman. I commit her to your loving care, beseeching you to receive her soul into the mercy of your love. Amen."

Did God hear Cesar's plea? Would He intervene and lead law-enforcement to her killer?

Cesar shook his head with doubt—this horrendous, bone-chilling crime would likely go unsolved. From experience, he knew the odds that ninety-eight percent of all missing person cases and murders in Mexico and Central America remained unsolved. Cesar now hoped that her loved ones *had* reported her missing. Even if this was the case, the chance of the missing senior being actively sought out was highly unlikely. Nevertheless, a thought did cross the agent's mind: *Was she a Mexican citizen, or born elsewhere in Central America, perhaps?*

As he headed for the inlet, Cesar's aspiration was that someone, somewhere, knew this aged woman and could shed some light on who she was, and, possibly, who might have killed her. Unknown to this sensitive, caring agent, there *was* someone, worried sick about this woman's absence—her daughter!

On this fateful early morning, Cesar's compassionate feelings for another human being failed to mask his pent-up pain of what had happened twenty-five years ago.

It was vile and unforgivable!

 glo

Cesar Luis Rivas, the oldest of three sons of documented Mexican immigrants, was born just outside the city limits of Laredo, Texas in 1962. His hard-working parents had several jobs to put the brightest of their three boys, Cesar, through community college. It was at this educational facility that the college's chief academic advisor offered Cesar the career option of a bachelor's degree in Criminal Justice.

But it didn't come to fruition as the ardent student had wished.

A few months into his dedicated studies, the student's world turned upside down in an instant. The unexpected, stomach-churning telephone call knocked the wind out of Cesar's sails. His father, Arnoldo, was dead, brutally stabbed to death in his own home.

It was very, very real.

That fateful summer's day in 1994 after working a ten-hour dayshift in a warehouse as a package handler for a major courier company, Arnoldo drove the twenty-five miles to his home, located on the outskirts of the City of Laredo. As he drove into the driveway, a shiver ran down his spine. Something was very wrong. His forehead stretched high as he noted that the front door was ajar and even more perplexed at the flashes glinting in the sunlight on the porch.

Without a second thought for his safety, Arnoldo alighted from his vehicle, navigated his footwear over broken panel glass around the entrance porch, and rushed into his home. Uneasiness flooded his being as he approached the kitchen. There, sitting at the kitchen table, was a young adult of average height with a shaven head. He looked to be about seventeen, the same age as his youngest son. Arnoldo watched in astonishment as the kid gulped down the meal his wife, Jessica, left for him. Something she usually did before departing for her nightshift as a cleaner at the local hospital. He recalled her words and her beautiful smile like a sunray: "There are fresh corn tamales in the fridge for you and the boys. And pozole soup is in the slow cooker. I love you, *cariño*. See you tomorrow morning."

"I love you, too," was Arnoldo's reply.

It would be his last spoken words to the woman he adored.

⚜

The affronted homeowner scowled at the heavily tattooed kid, who oozed creepiness. At this point, Arnoldo was still trying to unscramble astounded emotions. Then intuition nudged him to tread carefully, and so he checked the urge to shout at the invader. Arnoldo's calm voice reached out, *"Que estas haceindo.* What are you doing in my home? Who are you?"

"Someone you don't want to mess with!" was the threatening Spanish retort.

Arnoldo sized up the teen.

The symbolic neck tattoos identified him as a dangerous criminal gang member—Mara Salvatrucha (also known as MS-13), whose dictum was: Mata, Viola, Controla—Kill, Rape, Control. It was collective knowledge throughout the Laredo Hispanic community that a significant number of Salvadoran gang members had sought refuge in the United States during and now after the civil war.

Julio Luis Olivares junior, nicknamed, "Loco," was one of them.

The youngest of six children, Loco, came from a broken home. His father, Julio Olivares senior, an Army Private in the National

Guard, left for work one morning and never returned to the residence. No amount of questions: *"Where's my father?"* Or *"Where's my husband?"* brought answers to Olivares' disappearance. The military officials were keeping tight-lipped, casting a veil of secrecy over one of their own. Loco's family was devastated.

In the time that followed abandonment, worsening poverty wreaked havoc on the soldier's family. Loco's destitute mother took in laundry during the day, cleaning for elite families, and worked the nightshift in a garment factory, producing uniforms. Like the rest of the children, Loco was unable to attend public school because of worn-out clothing and lack of money. The eleven-year-old boy's attitude toward his remaining single parent took a turn for the worse. He grew emotionally unstable and indignantly withdrew from her and refused to obey her strict curfews. At every opportunity, Loco wandered the streets of Los Apoyos, a market town. It didn't take long in this high crime neighborhood for a lonely boy's vulnerability to come to the notice of the watchful eyes of crime "scouts" who preferred juveniles to adults for recruitment into the lucrative drug-smuggling trade. In the scouts' mindsets, Loco's damaged life needed recognition, belonging. And so this boy's mental fragility became a significant factor in agreeing to become a "mule" for organized crime bosses known for using such children. With the exciting potential of making up to $500 USD on a good day, more than a factory worker would make in four months, Loco was ready to take his first assignment. The thought of making such easy money overruled the genuine dangers of the world for this vulnerable "lost" boy. In Loco's "all grown up" demeanor, he was going to embark on the most exciting adventure he had since stepping out of diapers.

Or so the beguiled child thought!

∾⃟∾

One week later, with forged "*Cédulas de Indentidas*," the official ID travel permits, needed for border crossings between Central American countries, Loco, and two teenage companions traveled west by bus on the Pan-American Highway (the longest single road in the world, built with U.S. backing) into neighboring Guatemala. There, the boys were met by a cartel member, who gave the minors explicit verbal directives that they had to memorize. Satisfied that these newest mules are able to record orders mentally, the drug boss gave their protégés twenty US dollars each for bus fares, food, and the purchase of backpacks.

After several days of lengthy bus trips, the three "*droga la mula*" (drug smuggling mules) finally reached the Mexican city of Nuevo Laredo on the border with the United States. In the blazing heat of midday, they met up with the "packer."

With, three waterproof backpacks stuffed to the zippers with contraband the boy mules were instructed to hide out of sight in an abandoned building until nightfall. When given the "okay" by the contraband packer to exit the building, the trio swam across the Rio Grande in pitch darkness. The stealthy swimmers reached the other side and handed their backpacks, containing pouches of cocaine, over to the waiting contact. Loco couldn't believe it when he received his first paycheck of two-hundred US dollars. His immediate thought was to swim back, return to El Salvador and surprise his mother when she returned home in the morning from the factory. But hesitation followed. How would he explain his newfound wealth? Anna Olivares had, on many occasions, warned all of her children to have no association with the criminals that roamed the streets for easy prey.

A mother's sound advice had obviously fallen on deaf ears. Anna's youngest son never did return home. In time, Loco became just a "missing" child among hundreds of other missing youth in El Salvador.

◌

Preferring his nickname "Loco," he eventually ended up in Los Angeles, after undergoing numerous river crossings carrying contraband. He was inducted into the MS-13 gang affiliation and, was thrust deeper into criminal activity and gang violence. The undiagnosed and untreated teen with probable "dissociative identity disorder" believed he now had a sense of *connection*, that he was a grown man and, could no longer be pushed aside as if he was merely a worn-out shoe. This supposition was heightened by the abuse of alcohol, marijuana, and crack cocaine.

Loco's reign as a recognized gang member would be short-lived.

Five years later, Loco was rounded up by ICE (Immigration and Customs Enforcement-Bureau) and held in detention for thirty days, awaiting the quota to fill the "special" airplane owned by the U.S. government. The deportees, no longer the responsibility of the United States, and with no provisions made for them by the

El Salvadoran government, were *dumped* at San Salvador airport at midnight. Loco was, attired in usual gang member clothing: a blue plaid shirt worn loosely and untucked with wide-legged jeans sagging around hips. On his broad feet were, pricey Nike Cortez footwear, which attested to what was a life of financial means, until now.

Loco and the other passengers found themselves back in their country without any official identification. At customs, Loco's bogus ID was confiscated. Without a dime in his pocket, Loco followed the other deportees through immigration exit doors and then headed for the streets he knew well. Within a few days, Loco went back to the old ways way of making quick money—drug trafficking. It didn't take long to sink back into the swing of things, making lots of money. The drug addict's firm resolve was that when the opportunity presented itself, he'd make his way back into the United States.

He did just that a year later.

Chapter Three

The Rivas Home, Laredo, Texas

- BACKTRACKED TO 1994 -

"There are many things worth living for, a few things worth dying for, and nothing worth killing for."
—TOM ROBBINS

Inside Arnoldo's family home, bravado replaced fear. Arnoldo's voice was now under tight control, ready for a pitch-fork attack. He said in disgust and rage, "Get the hell out of my house! How dare you break into my home, eat my food, drink my beer, and think you can get away with it? I guess that you are probably illegal. I'm calling the police."

Arnoldo's threat failed to impress the lanky gang member. Loco smirked, "I'm chilling out with this *sabroso* (tasty) food. Damn it, old man. Can't you buy better beer then this American crap? It tastes like piss." Loco casually adjusted the black bandana wrapped around his forehead and then rose from the table. He reached down the back of the band of his pants and, whipped out a steel weapon. Waving the blade in Arnoldo's direction, Loco menacingly demanded, "Hand over your wallet, your watch, and your wedding ring. I assume it is gold?"

Arnoldo was more than furious at the audacity of this young thug. He was not giving in to this machete-wielding teenager with soulless eyes. In his mindset, he had the right to protect himself in his own home.

A torrent of survival adrenalin surged through the man's body as he darted for the foot-long blade hidden near a kitchen dresser. A couple of inches off grabbing the weapon, Arnoldo slipped on the polished floor and landed, with a thud.

What happened next is unimaginable.

Loco moved in and, with a blitz attack, viciously attacked the recumbent Arnoldo. Half this boy's size, and physically weak from a lung infection, Arnoldo never stood a chance as he sustained deep cuts to his chest, head, and neck. One stab wound to his heart ended his life. Following the brutal attack, the heartless assailant removed the cash from Arnoldo's wallet as he bled out. It had fallen out of a trouser pocket during the attack. Then the pitiless young adult wrenched-off Arnoldo's watch and wedding ring. With a satisfied sneer crossing his lips, Arnoldo's assailant opened the back door and fled on foot through the heavily wooded area behind the residence without being seen.

❦

Shortly after 6:00 p.m., Arnoldo's two younger sons returned from their respective factory workplaces and stumbled upon the horrific scene. Everything froze. It was like their world turned black. With one eye open and one closed (an indication that his death had come swiftly) laid the body of their beloved head of the family. Arnoldo's last-born son's body shook convulsion while the other son checked for a pulse. There was none. The 911 call from the landline was fraught, "Come quick," the sobbing voice requested. "My father has been murdered."

Sirens blared. The Rivas residence lit up with the blue and red flashing strobe lights of a patrol car. A police officer stepped inside the house, and trained eyes examined the bloody crime scene. The law-enforcement officer immediately radioed for backup. Within minutes, yellow and black crime scene tape flapped in a lively gust of wind around the Rivas home. Inside the residence, the CSI was hard at work, collecting available evidence. The elite team of crime scene investigators tagged and then bagged a beer can, the blood-stained machete, and lifted a fingerprint off the refrigerator and front door.

Shortly after, Arnoldo's lifeless body was removed from the somber residence and, an all-out search for the unknown assailant whose clothing, if not discarded, would be saturated in Arnoldo's blood began.

A K-9 handler and his German Shepherd, Kato, were deployed. The officer and his tracker dog with 200 million scent-receptor cells, his nose on the ground, instantly picked up the scent trail left by Loco. Handler and sleuth-hound sprinted like a long-distance runner in pursuit of Arnoldo's killer. The dog followed Loco's scent through dense woods to a fast-flowing stream where the hunt for the killer ended. Loco had made a successful escape for now.

Days, weeks, months, and then years went by.

Having exhausted all leads to follow up on, and with no further possible witnesses to interview or evidence to collect and analyze, the murder of Arnoldo Rivas officially closed, slipping into the Cold Files. His brutal murder was now nothing more than a pile of paperwork placed in a box on a shelf, marked: ARNOLDO LUIS RIVAS-COLD CASE FILE-11089-1994, but not forgotten.

Arnoldo's attacker had gotten away with murder, for now. Will the devastated Rivas family have closure to this torture of not knowing?

৩৹

Cesar was frustrated to learn about the decision to place the case in storage, but he wasn't giving up this readily. He dropped into the Laredo police department regularly, begging them to reopen his father's case. His constant visits, along with numerous telephone calls, became fruitless. However, something was productive following the murder of his father. Homeowners in the neighborhood changed their behaviors by, locking doors, arming themselves, and also acquiring fearsome-looking guard dogs. The residents now looked out for each other during the day and night. This new protective behavior couldn't have helped the devastated Rivas family. Would this shattered family ever know what the motivation was for the brutal murder of a beloved father, a source of unfailing strength and love who was a role model, telling his sons that they could be anything they wanted to do?

One day, in the future.

Back in 1994, the lead investigator on the Rivas case had a bulldog personality. Homicide Det. Carlos Sandoval promised the heartbroken family, "No matter how long it takes, I'm not going to stop looking for your father's killer." He continued in a voice like bottled thunder, "I'm going to nail the bastard. You mark my words."

From then on, this dedicated investigator sacrificed most of his personal life, working ten to twelve hours a day but coming up empty. He would receive his first real break after a telephone call from a jailhouse informer, twenty-five years later.

"I want to make a deal," the male caller said. "I know who killed an old man in Texas."

With DNA technology, Det. Sandoval would ultimately bring Arnoldo's killer to justice. The blueprinting of life, DNA (the genetic biochemistry information in cells), would eventually become the *voice* of murdered victims.

After his father's murder, Cesar's life did an about-turn. His dreams of becoming a criminal prosecutor ended on that day in 1994. But this was the least of his concerns. It was his mother's suicidal outburst that wrenched his heart from his chest. Norma Rivas wrung her hands, and limpid, tear-filled eyes met her son. "I wish I were dead. I don't want to live without your father, the only man I have ever loved. You boys are old enough to take care of yourselves."

"Mother, please don't say that," Cesar implored. "We love and need you and will take care of you."

Later, while his mother slept soundly under sedation, and Cesar's traumatized brothers passed out from an excess of tequila, Arnoldo's first-born son was overcome with avenging thoughts that he did not wish to share with anyone—like finding his father's killer and strangling him to death. What had taken place in his home devoured Cesar's fragile psyche. He had to protect his loved ones. So, after his father's burial service, Cesar got into top physical shape. Then he enrolled in the Border Patrol Academy, undergoing the law enforcement courses and rigorous fitness training programs. Nineteen weeks later, Cesar graduated from the top of his class. Now Border Patrol Agent Rivas was ready to defend his country from the likes of "Loco" and others who might think that their criminal activities would go unpunished.

Like the character in a popular comic book, *The Punisher*, a new role with a helluva grudge, was unleashed to fight crime.

Border Agent Cesar Rivas was that man.

Chapter Four

At the Rio Grande Crime Scene

- AUGUST 2019 -

*"No crime of this heinous nature can ever be
defended rationally in a courtroom."*
—Unknown

Before uttering a final prayer for the deceased, Cesar stood by the body of the elderly deceased dwarf, who was about the same size as his five-year-old daughter conceived late in life, perplexed thoughts brought Rivas to question again: *Who was this person who had met such a violent end?*

"Damn bastards!" he cussed, swatting off a swarm of mosquitos that were, attracted to the carbon dioxide of the deceased woman's flesh. "Alive or dead, these rotten pests have no mercy."

Having returned to the site, Dwayne nodded. "Damn scuzzballs are active tonight for sure. I have repellent spray in the vehicle. I'll go and get it. Not that it will be much help to her, but *we* sure can use it."

Alone, Cesar's caring, tender heart sprang into action. He removed his jacket and covered the lifeless woman. At this very moment, another brutal murder became vivid. Cesar shook his head vigorously, trying to shake off *that* reflection. But it could never be that easy. His father's horrific demise and that of this little person would have a profound effect on the rest of his natural life.

⌖

Headlights on full beam lit up the riverbank area, like a football stadium. The County Sheriff immediately sealed off the area. The murder victim was placed in a body bag and then transported away by the coroner for autopsy, along with several items of clothing washed ashore.

Unanswered questions for all involved dangled in the air: *Did the washed-up clothing belong to the victim, or simply lost by another illegal crossing this dangerous river? If the clothing did belong to the victim, would they find trace evidence?*

The coroner notified the little person's body departed into the custody of the Laredo County Coroner Office for assessment of the cause and manner of death.

⌖

After the crime scene became still from noise, Cesar had a troubling question that he addressed aloud, "I wonder if this homicide happened in Mexico or the United States."

"Good question," Dwayne responded.

Deep down, Cesar also wondered: *Would the victim speak from the realm of the dead at the autopsy?*

Absolutely!

Unknown to the individuals involved in her recovery, this little person was born with extraordinary abilities, the remarkable power, spiritually sensitive to the energies of the living and the dead.

⚬⟊⟊

At the medical examiner's office, the final cause of death ruling would be undertaken by Doctor Morgana Saeger, an expert pathologist who had performed over three thousand autopsies of whom many were *illegals* that had washed up with such frequency. However, *this* forensic autopsy would be an uphill battle for the doctor. Trying to obtain fingerprints from the victim's deeply wrinkled epidermis was virtually impossible. But Morgana wasn't to be thwarted. She began the voice-recorded examination of the body lying on the cold steel table. Articulately, she spoke, "Ropes bind the victim's arms and legs. Sharp impact injuries are visible—" A loud exhalation ended the sentence. For over forty years, she had been the voice of the dead and thought nothing could shock her. But it did.

Forty-eight hours following the autopsy, Morgana Saeger released her Summary Autopsy Report.

Her professional findings were chilling:

DATE AND HOUR OF FULL AUTOPSY

PERFORMED by Morgana Saeger, M.D.
ASSISTED by Michelle Jackson M.D.
2333 Zapata Hwy
Laredo, TX 78046
956-726-8666
August 14 2019 - 8:30 a.m.

SUMMARY REPORT OF AUTOPSY

Name:	Coroner's Case #:
JANE DOE	2019-299
Date of Birth:	Age:
UNKNOWN	50's to 60's
Race:	Sex:
HISPANIC	FEMALE
Date of Death:	Body Identified by:
Estimated at being between	UNIDENTIFIED
11 and 12 of August 2019	

Case #   Investigative Agency
001282-23B-2019   Laredo County Sheriff's Department

EXTERNAL EXAMINATION:

The recorded autopsy began at 8:30 a.m. on August 14, 2019.

"The body is presented in a black body bag. The victim was naked. Extra-large male clothing found at the scene does not belong to the victim. No jewelry is present."

"The body is a Latina female, an adult dwarf, measuring 4 feet tall and weighing 122 lbs. Her facial symmetry and increased head circumference are consistent with dwarfism. Lividity is fixed in distal portions of the limbs. Her eyes are open. Irises are dark brown, and corneas are cloudy. Petechial hemorrhaging is present in the conjunctival surfaces of her eyes. There is a small amount of crustacean mutilation."

"Upturned nose with hypoplasia of the nasal bridge is consistent with dwarfism."

"Hair color is pewter-gray, wavy, and approximately five inches in length at the longest point. Fingernails are abraded, and fingernail beds are blue. She has opaque twelve upper and five lower teeth, which indicates a probable history of enamel deficiency, possibly from childhood malnutrition. The tone of the epidermal skin is pale and edematous, abnormally swollen, which shows slow decomposition underwater."

"I note the presence of several unexplained surface bruises. There are no tattoos."

"There are, in total, fifty stab post-mortem wounds, seemingly violent, to the breasts, stomach, chest, neck, and shoulder consistent with crimes of passion. There are no defensive wounds to the victim's hands."

"Dark red ligature marks encircle wrists, consistent with being rope tied. There is genital trauma, lacerations, with injury patterns of the upper vagina, associated with sexual assault. Vaginal and anal swabs are in evidence."

"Embedded in the right frontal area of the skull is a piece of metal from a sharp weapon, unidentified at this time. It speaks of an intense bludgeoning."

"There is an injury to thyroid cartridge by strangulation. Also, present a recent nasal bone fracture over the bridge of the victim's nose."

"The manner of death is extreme homicidal violence."

"I've been informed that the area surrounding the crime scene was thoroughly combed, but nothing has been found, no connecting murder weapon."

"I've narrowed down the death timeline to approximately twenty-four hours by the gases of bloating decomposition, increasing buoyancy, which allows a deceased body to float to the surface. It is unlikely with such injuries that the victim was alive when placed in the water."

INTERNAL EXAMINATION:

HEAD: "X-rays show a fractured hyoid bone above the larynx, nasal bone, and skull fracture from the impact of sharp object.

"Hemorrhaging from strangulation is present the skin and subdermal tissues of the neck.

"The brain weighs 1,303 grams and is within normal limits."

SKELETAL SYSTEM: "The hyoid bone is fractured."

RESPIRATORY SYSTEM: "Petechial hemorrhaging is present in the lips and oral cavity.

"The lungs weigh: right, 355 grams; left 362. The lungs are unremarkable. Drowning is ruled out."

CARDIOVASCULAR SYSTEM: "The heart weighs 253 grams, of average size, and has been punctured in the right ventricle."

URINARY SYSTEM: "The kidneys weigh: left, 115 grams; right 113 grams. The kidneys are generally anatomic in size, shape, and location, but are punctured."

STOMACH: "The stomach is empty of gastric content."

LIVER: "The liver weighs 1500 grams. No liver disease found."

FEMALE GENITAL SYSTEM: "Examination of the pelvic area indicates the victim has given birth, is not pregnant at the time of death. There is evidence of forced sexual activity. Vaginal fluid samples removed for analysis."

CONCLUSION: "Rigor and livor mortis conclude the approximate the time of death between 7:30 and 9:30 a.m., on the 11 or 12 of this month, August, 2019. Immediate cause of death is: "Asphyxia by ligature strangulation. Stab wounds are post-mortem. No weapon was found at the crime scene. The morphology of the wounds is consistent with a double-edged knife such as a Bowie."

REMARKS:

"I've ruled out drowning, no extra fluid in the deceased's lungs. Jane Doe's death is ruled a homicide."
Morgana Saeger, M.D.
Laredo County Coroner's Office
August 14, 2019

What the doctor did not record at this autopsy were personal thoughts: *How long would it take to identify the victim, give her a name? Who was responsible for this brutal act of violence? Can justice ever be served?*

∽∾

On this day, and after a full day's work, and in the privacy of her own home, Morgana did record her feelings in a journal:

> *"Only crime and the criminal,*
> *it is true, confront us with*
> *the perplexity of evil . . ."*

Morgana hoped that the culprit responsible for this heinous murder would be caught, arrested, and prosecuted. She could only desire it to be soon. However, the caring doctor knew from experience that it would be almost impossible with so many illegals rarely reported as missing. Nevertheless, she had ensured that DNA evidence was collected. Could it one day unlock the secrets to this brutal murder? If so, there could be no defense argument. In this doctor's professional opinion, this remarkable science *is* the wrongdoer's undoing.

∽∾

Later, as Morgana soaked in the bathtub, her thoughts began wandering like a desert nomad. She couldn't get the little person's twisted face off her mind or the look in open eyes. Had she known her killer? Her internal dialogue continued: *Who was this little person?*

Why had she met such a violent death?

⚜

Sadly, Dr. Morgana Saeger would not learn the identity of Jane Doe, whom she had so much empathy for. Because, three weeks after performing the autopsy, she died in a hit and run collision two miles from her place of work.

The habitual drunk driver finally apprehended was convicted of first-degree homicide by vehicle and sentenced to life without the possibility of parole.

At least one woman received justice. As for the little person, her time to receive the same justice was long in the making.

Chapter Five

El Salvador

- NOVEMBER 1969 -

*"Even the smallest person can change
the course if the future."*
—J.R.R. TOLKIEN

In a field on the outskirts of the village of Masahaut, she sat on bare buttocks in a loamy soil. Born in 1966, the four-year-old girl, in a faded brown dress, was smaller than the 18-inch oval-leafed herbaceous plant her short torso and wide feet straddled. With determination, little fingers grappled the base of the groundnut plant, to uproot it from its underground nest. No matter how hard she tugged, the pods clustered around the base of the root remained stubborn. The child with a protruding jaw cried out, "Mamá, come and help!"

Fifty-one-year-old, Analena, lowered the hessian sack of collected peanuts strapped on her back and laid it on the ground. She headed toward her child. Born with achondroplasia (dwarfism), she'd named her Estrella, for her moon-shaped large head.

Was gene mutation inherited? Was the mother a carrier of metabolic and hormonal disorders, such as growth hormone deficiency?

Estrella's deformity had torn out a piece out of her mother's heart, causing unbearable conflict in her state of mind. Analena was sure God had punished her. Four years ago, she had informed the local priest that she no longer wanted to practice the sermons of the Roman Catholic Church: "Be fruitful and multiply." Gen: 1:28

The parish priest's immediate response was, "Analena, not having more children is a selfish choice."

His direct statement rubbed the usually passive Analena Godwin Lozano the wrong way. Her body shook in retaliatory frustration as she answered, "I have already given the Lord twelve Christian souls. Two of whom *He* took in premature deaths. How can He not understand that every day is getting harder and harder to provide for my children who live? They go to bed at night, bellies grumbling from hunger. As you well know, my father, my husband, and I make very little money from sharecropping. It barely covers the necessities of life, not to mention the donation to the church that you collect after each harvest time. No, I refuse to allow my husband to lie down with me."

The priest's facial muscles twitched as if an electrical current was passing through him. "God will punish you for this selfish decision," he sniped. "I will pray for the redemption of your soul."

(The Roman Catholic Church teaches birth control is okay, as long as it involves nothing like condoms, pills, etc. In the early twentieth century, the calendar-base method known as the rhythm method was promoted by members of the Catholic Church as the only morally acceptable form of family planning). Is this brain-washing or merely a form of malignant narcissism?

⚛

Since her outspoken spate with the pompous priest, Analena deprived her husband of a romp in the hay. Unless—

The cost of a condom was a full day's pay!

But a bombshell awaited Analena. She didn't know that new "life" had snuggled in her womb four days before the angry confrontation with the priest. Child number thirteen was on the way!

Will folklore symbolism bring bad luck or misfortune? The question was: lucky or unlucky number 13? The ancient Aztecs considered thirteen to be a very sacred number. In the Bible, 26 numbers (written in the cardinal form) are multiples of 13. Spiritually, it is the weight of the soul, in an ounce. Did Analena Lozano, born on Friday 13 1918, in the Amazon Rainforest, even believe in luck? Nope!

Chapter Six

Ecuador's Gateway to the Amazon Rainforest

- EARLY OCTOBER 191 8 -

"Society is still not a civilization.
It is still primitive and barbaric."
—SWAMI D. GITEN

The name *"Amazon"* was given to the region by the Spanish explorer Francisco Orellana after female warriors attacked him named the *Icamiabas*—women without husbands.

The Amazon River Basin, cradled by the Andes Mountains, provides access to the biodiverse Amazon Rainforest, over seven million square kilometers (roughly the size of Australia). The rainforest, referred to as being "The Lungs of the Earth" consumes approximately twenty-five percent of atmospheric carbon dioxide. This tropical kingdom of forests, so full of mystery and danger, sustained an abundance of life. An array of magical jungle giant trees, exotic and poisonous plants, macaw parrots, the jaguar, sloth and river dolphins, anacondas, amphibians such as the lethal dart frog and anacondas. It was also "home" to the illusive Waorani Indians, permanent forest settlers, never seen by outsiders. Comparable to most Amazonian natives, this Stone-Age tribe was highly empathetic with their wildlife-rich environment, close to nature, giving reverence to fertile earth. The natives believed that trees housed the spirits of their ancestors. They would go to any length to appease them. So on this October day, the odor from sodden earth that followed heavy precipitation, was perfume to all nostrils. The jungle forest—, hot, humid, and wet all year round—, provided an abundance of açai berries, and other wild fruits.

The formidable warriors of the rainforest still fiercely guard *their* territory, earning a reputation for savagery. Until now, they had not made contact with the outsiders, who were, in their perception the mortal "enemy."

On this October day, the elusive Waorani will become challenged by the arrival of strangers, American evangelists, with a Protestant allegiance dating to the sixteenth century Italian reform movement. With fundamental purpose, woven by religious fervor, evangelists preached the teachings of Jesus Christ to atheists. The self-appointed altruists had traveled to South America with the notion that they could "tame" the primitive Amazonians. .

But do-gooders underestimated the intelligence of the congenital natives: "Primitive does not mean stupid." It was only the beginning of misconceptions, basically ignorance.

Subsequently, this Friday, what begins with expectation for the American altruists bearing gifts of machetes and aluminum kettles, to win trust, ends in unimaginable terror.

Before their intrusive arrival, at sunrise, a fourteen-year-old, diminutive teen, four-foot-two inches in height, almost pigmy, named Kayapa, removed her pubic hair by first rubbing ash in the area, and then methodically pulled out the hairs. Satisfied that not a single hair remained, the pregnant girl, as instructed by her mother, began boiling water to make *ayahuasca*, a traditional tea made from the Psychotria Viridis shrub and shredded stalks of the caapi vine. This sacred beverage was not only used for spiritual purposes but as a calming effect to pain-free birthing. Once the beverage cooled, Kayapa's mother strained the highly concentrated liquid to remove impurities and poured the liquid into a clay vessel. She instructed, "Drink my daughter, and all will be well this day."

Kayapa's face puckered with the sour-tasting concoction. She gagged to keep the brew down. Her mother reached for her daughter's clammy hand. Clasping it gently, she urged, "Go now and *quickly*," she emphasized, "and bring your first baby to life. Your grandmother, whose spirit lives in a La Lupuna birthing tree, came to me in a dream last night. She told me the El Tunchi (revered tree spirits) forewarned her that bad people are coming to suck out the blood from our bodies before this day is out. So once your baby is born, we must flee deeper into the forest."

Kayapa didn't like this ominous message and, with urgency, hurried away from the communal dwelling.

As was the native custom, she sought out a tree, a quiet place deep in the middle of the twilight forest. With less than one percent of light making it through the canopy of the tree, she squatted between the twisted roots of the giant 200-feet high La Lupuna tree. And six hours later, she birthed her daughter, without attendance or sound. It was a natural first birth, thanks to her mother's traditional concoction. The new mother placed her newborn offspring on her tummy, cut the umbilical cord with a sharp rock, crushed the pulsating flesh, and buried it along with the attached placenta. This centuries-old ritual handed down in gratitude for the abundance of edible food, such as beetle grubs, palm hearts, and wild legumes, and the tribe's main diet of Marmoset monkeys gave, them all the nutrition needed.

The afternoon sun positioned high in the sky, and humidity levels at their highest, the nursing mother, her newborn to a breast, began making her way back to the temporary home on the riverbank, a communal shack built from rough timbers and covered in palm fronds.

Brilliant crimson body paint from crushed berries, adorned her face, complemented by facial piercings designed from thin bamboo strips, and fist-size balsa hoops in her elongated earlobes. With these beauty adornments flapping against her neck, Kayapa sprinted to present the baby to its father, (a first cousin), when suddenly the forest became shattered by shrill resonances, never before created by any forest beast she knew. She had an uneasy feeling.

Suddenly, Kayapa's legs turned to rubber. Her heart pounding in ears, Kayapa's flight responses kicked in. She dashed for cover behind lush groundcover of riverside vegetation. Something just didn't sit right with this "gifted" girl, born with the exceptional ability to perceive things that are usually beyond the range of most human senses.

Muscles tense, and jaws locked, Kayapa peered out blearily

from her hide-out. Were the after-effects of ayahuasca playing tricks with her mind? She just didn't know what to make of *pale* people, never seen before. Gifted-instinct told the young mother that life would not be the same again. In front of her, near the river's edge, a threatening situation was unfolding.

The Waorani menfolk, twenty in number, with gourds tied around waists, razor-sharp housing blow-darts dipped in curare (culturally termed "flying death") propelled from seven-foot-long blowguns, quickly and wordlessly, encircled the missionaries.

Women and children were nowhere in sight. Like Olympic athletes, they had sprinted deep into the camouflaged forest.

Kayapa continued to watch with eyesight coming into focus.

Seemingly, unafraid of the hostile postures, Preacher Josiah Godwin placated in English, "We come in peace and wish you no harm. We are missionaries. We come to preach the gospels of the New Testament…"

The tall, slim evangelist, in his late forties, was cut short by his wife, who stepped out in from of him. Using American Sign Language believed to be understood through most eyes, was backed up in her native Spanish tongue, "We have brought gifts to show good intent."

Blank guarded stares answered her.

Thirty-seven-year-old, Belicia Analena Medena Godwin, gestured to the wooden crates that had been hurriedly dumped by the boat owner, whose alarmed expression was plain to read: *"I'm getting the hell out of here."* His nervous body language was not taken seriously by this American family.

ᑯᑋᓷ

The day before this goodwill excursion to the jungle, word had spread around Mompiche, an isolated Ecuadorian fishing village that foreign missionaries wished to hire a boat to travel to the Amazon rainforest so that they could bring the word of God to the heathens. A desperately poor fisherman, as most in this small village were, jumped at the chance of quick money-making. In his late sixties, the grey-haired man swiftly made his way to the only hotel in the town where the foreigners were staying. He found them sitting out on the hotel terrace drinking tea and addressed the Americans in his best English, "I am Adelmo, I own a boat big enough to transport all of you, but it won't be cheap."

Belicia answered in Spanish, "Money is no object, Señor Adelmo."

Adelmo smiled with relief. "Your Spanish is good, Señora."

She smiled warmly. "Well, it should be. Spanish is my first language, Señor Adelmo. I was born in Central America."

Adelmo beamed, happy to learn he wouldn't have to struggle with a language he didn't know or even like. Now highly delighted with the traveling arrangements, a large sum of "Sucre" (currency at this time) exchanged hands.

Would Christian society's brainwashing work for primitive life? Or would "imposed" religious doctrines become merely birds of ill omens?

ᑯᑋᓷ

Early the next morning, Friday the 13th as arranged, Adelmo met up with his passengers outside the hotel. The boat owner's bushy gray eyebrows arched upwards. He wasn't sure if what he was seeing was real! The live-for-today Adelmo didn't know whether to laugh or cry.

There they were, garbed ready for a social, dressy function!

Josiah and the boys wore striped double-breasted suits and matching vests, high white collar dress shirts, decked by black ties. Lace-up boots, plus straw-boaters atop their black hair, were their "practical" gear. But it was Belicia's attire that made Adelmo scratch his head in disbelief.

Josiah's Godwin's plump wife was wearing a white lacy blouse and red skirt, the hemline slightly above ankles exposing high button boots. Accompanying her unsuitable outfit were white wrist-length elegant gloves. Wrapped loosely around her neck, a red silk scarf fluttered in a breeze. Adelmo couldn't help but grin. But he did note that she was a beautiful, sophisticated woman who had a flawless complexion. Her cascading black hair brushed back was tied in a bun at the nape of her neck. Her most striking characteristic was her dark-brown eyes that could have melted snow. He also noted that Belicia was having difficulty breathing at 2,800 meters above sea level air. She greeted the boat owner in a raspy voice, "Good morning, Señor Adelmo. We are ready as we will ever be to do God's work."

"God has indeed sent you," Adelmo stated. "And may God also protect you," the devout Catholic man ended sincerely.

Within the hour, the wooden boat's hull splashed through turbulent waters of the Napo River, a waterway that merged other waterways to form the mighty Amazon River, providing entry into the rainforest. Adelmo was to deliver his passengers to the earlier observed riverside camp. But the old fisherman wasn't sure that it would still be there.

It was common knowledge throughout South America that Amazonian natives were always on the move as hunter-gatherers for game such as deer, monkey, and tapir. When the rivers flowed slowly, they fished. As luck had it, the palm-thatched huts *were* still there. But not a jungle dweller was visible, although Adelmo *felt* their presence. He knew their survival tactics—to stay one step ahead of potential harm from outsiders and concealing themselves by coating mud on their naked bodies, slapping twigs, grass, and other vegetation from the forest floor onto this covering a natural camouflage, so that they blended into the woodland background.

⚬⎰⎱⚬

The anxious, lip-biting Adelmo steered his boat ashore conscious of the "untamed" history of savage tribes, whom he thought was probably observing their every move from behind jungle foliage. The scared man wanted *out* fast. Drop them off and get the hell out from this dangerous territory was his intention. Reading Adelmo's nervous body language, Josiah spoke up, "We will be just fine. Don't worry, Señor."

Two wooden crates, and personal luggage, were put on the ground. Adelmo had one last thing to do. "Good luck and God bless. I hope everything goes well. As arranged, I'll be back for you in one week. If you intend to stay longer, fasten a blue cloth to a rock on the shore. Then I'll know your stay is productive, and if you wish to remain longer..." Adelmo then gestured to Belicia's red scarf. "Leave *that* in plain sight, if there is an emergency," he ended sketchily. He was a decent man, he told himself, but just the thought of having to come back to this godforsaken place wasn't an option. Anyway, he had been paid well in advance, once-in-a-lifetime exorbitant earnings, for both proposed trips.

The family glanced at the lightweight boat as Adelmo made a hasty getaway into the choppy waters. "Adios, Adelmo," they said in unison. Josiah added, "Thank you for bringing us here. God will reward you."

"We'll see you again as arranged, Adelmo," said the oldest Godwin son.

Frenzied oars beat the water in a hasty retreat. Adelmo prayed, "Querido Dios, por favor, protect these people of your Word."

Suspicious, and hostile gazes, focused on the uninvited visitors as they moved out into the open. "Hello," the family greeted warmly, making their way to the Indians. "We are happy to meet you."

With austere cultures and language barriers clashing, the Waorani's chief, a formidable-looking stout, five-foot-tall man with a face tattooed in red plant dye and cheek and chin piercings, stomped forward. His face was bristling like porcupine quills. The leader responded in Waorani tongue, "You're not welcome, strange *woyera* (white) people! Leave our jungle homeland at once and never return!"

This grave warning wasn't understood. And so Josiah's oldest son, twenty-one-year-old, Jude, reached out, "We are here to teach you…"

Wrong move!

With heads high and challenging, and eyeballs blazing red with intensity, the Waorani glared at the intruders. Their leader's warning became surreal, "Leave our forest home *NOW!*"

Still unable to comprehend, Josiah reached into his trouser pocket and pulled out a shiny, polished object. The representation of the crucified Jesus Christ, held in direct sunlight, cast reflective laser-like beams onto warrior's faces.

That did it!

The Waorani didn't need western music. They began dancing to the beat of their hearts. Their "warrior-thumping" feet beat the ground as a countermanding force against what they believed to be "white" witchcraft as, they advanced. Josiah sensed danger but kept a cool head about him as he said, "Please, we wish no harm. We come in peace. We have brought gifts."

Suspicious tension continued to mount a hundredfold. With lips pressed together, the angry feet pounded the ground.

Ignorantly, the missionaries were not worried—their God would protect them. Josiah Godwin had been raised not to be a "giver-upper." So, extending the open hand of friendship, he moved closer. "We want to be your friends, not your enemies."

Painted foreheads raised high and catlike sharpness of combatant pupils, glinting like the crucifix, the Waorani leader's expression was: *Not ever going to happen!* Then at the flick of a switch, the tribal leader shouted, "Strike!"

Nothing said was understood by these missionaries. But it

didn't take long for the giant red flag to be raised, signaling real intent. Plant-dyed hands reached into waist gourds. Now realizing that something was about to go awry, the evangelists' fears became all too real.

This well-intended mission was about to become their worst nightmare: immediately, instinctive self-preservation set in. The Godwin family wanted to run, but their limbs were paralyzed with fear. Racing pulses beating in their ears, blocking out all other sounds. Terror became an alarming living force. Josiah fell to his knees, loudly beseeching, "GOD PROTECT US!" His shrill cry pierced nature, sending jungle creatures, large and small into a hasty retreat. Then all hell let loose.

The poisonous darts, aimed by skilled marksmen, flew into the air, fast and furious. With looks of sheer terror expressed on blood-drained features and screams that tore through their throats, the sharp barbs pierced their bodies. It was their anguished blood-curdling cries that had earlier halted Kayapa in her tracks.

As chilling as it may be, with this cold-blooded execution, the lack of empathy by the perpetrators would be considered criminal to the outside world, but not the inner workings of primordial blueprinting. For centuries, the Amazonian natives adopted this justification: *We better kill them before they kill us.*

James Russell Lowell's quote says it all:

"All thoughts that mold the age begins deep down within a primitive soul."

The five males, with punctured lungs suffocating them to death, made dying gurgles. The preacher's wife, Belicia, a citizen of Central America and America, had "doged the bullet" by purportedly skilled marksmen. A blow-dart had lodged in a hip bone, not a vital organ. Even so, why had she not succumbed to the deadly poison, curare?

Was it Divine intervention?

Doubtful!

⚬|⚬

After the multiple projectiles had found their targets, the Waorani fled deep into the jungle. One tribe member did not join them. Kayapa's bare feet, light as thistledown crept towards the campsite. She could see no living presence. However, at the periphery of her vision, she did see the "shadow beings" — dark humanoid figures, supernatural entities from a parallel dimension. Instinctively she knew that her human eyes weren't fooling her. These entities desired blood, and without it, couldn't be reborn. From ancient culture teaching passed down, she also believed that when the spirit of a human being becomes separated from its physical body by a violent death, an angry shadow entity will remain behind as the walking dead—zombies.

Kayapa's mother's words echoed in the flashback: "Your grandmother came to me in my sleep and told me—"

In the girl's psychic mindset, El Tunchi had brought bad people, who were now dead. No spiritual light emanated, which was a concern.

Among the Waorani culture, "*possession*" the inhabiting of a mortal being, is a common belief. Also, restless dead people could physically harm the living as La Mancha Mama had once told her. Although capable of challenging supernatural powers, young Kayapa wasn't going to let the dead, crying out to be avenged, inhabit *her* mortal being. "Leave this earth immediately," she commanded. "There is no place here on our land for white demons…"

A feeble voice broke into her words, "Please, help me."

Kayapa's short legs took flight.

The late afternoon sun cast long shadows over footprint impressions on the forest floor, bringing them to sharper relief. Using her forest-developed senses, Kayapa, clutching her crying baby, followed the human tracks through vegetation pushed aside into unnatural positions, in search of her people. She took note of the damaged twigs, fragmented cobwebs, and trampled grass. Kayapa walked onward, briefly stopping to quench her thirst with rainwater collected on the broad leaves. Without warning, her wetted lips froze. There was no mistaking the low, growling sound of a large cat, resonating through boughs. Afraid, Kayapa and her baby huddled under the treetop canopies that shaded most of the daylight. She stroked the thick trunk of a Kapok tree and softly supplicated, "La Mancha Mama, mother spirit of the jungle, you must protect me from the animal who kills in one leap and wishes to eat my baby and me." Seconds later, Kayapa stared into the pair of red glowing eyes. Mysteriously the jungle creature, with its trichromatic vision, failed to see its potential prey. La Mancha Mama had heard Kayapa's request and rendered her invisible to the eyes of the four-legged predator. Confident now that she wasn't going to become a nighttime snack, Kayapa gave thanks, "Good spirit, thank you for your protection. And now, quickly guide me to my people."

She once more followed along the footprints on the path. A few minutes later, she heard a familiar voice call out, "Kayapa, my daughter, you have found us."

The relieved girl followed her mother to their new home deep in the rainforest. There, Kayapa proudly presented her newborn daughter to fellow women. Though daughters are wholly accepted, Kayapa's sixteen-year-old partner showed little interest. "Wife, I'm happy that you have returned safely, but I have more pressing concerns to deal with now." With that brusquely said, the young warrior left his partner's side to join other men, grouped in a circle in a jungle clearing.

A heated discussion amongst the men began:

"Before this night hides the earth of light, we must return to the river and burn the huts," imparted the Waorani chieftain.

"And then we must hang the dead, as is our custom," another added.

"I agree," the leader voiced. "We must offer up the dead invaders, who brought dishonor to our lives, and our revered tree spirits."

A very young warrior contributed, "Why not just let the jungle beasts feast this night?"

The leader scowled at him. "It is not our custom!" he retorted irately.

Kayapa listened to this bantering and had a concern that she must share. She hesitantly entered the circle of Waorani men, which was forbidden—women meddling in warrior affairs were unheard of. Hands clasped to hips, Kayapa spilled forth the truth: "The unwelcome people are *not* all dead! The fat woman *is* alive. She called out to me, and I feel her pain tingling through my body."

The leader stared at her with doubt crossing his mind. "This cannot be," he disputed. "It was *my* flying death arrows that entered her body. Curare *never* fails to bring about death from many arrows!"

Kayapa pulled a face. "I'm telling the truth."

Her husband, Katanga, spoke up in her defense, "My wife has the mindreading powers of the ancient tree spirits. We all know La Mancha Mama is her guardian." Katanga was mindful that his outspokenness could have resulted in being banished from the tribe. No Waorani man argued with the leader.

As luck would have it, the leader nodded his head in total acceptance. "Yes, Katanga, you are right! She is *indeed* gifted." He faced Kayapa, "You must come with us, find the woman, and I'll make swift her death."

The men left the clearing with Kayapa in tow.

Pine-knot torches illuminated the marshaling darkness.

As intended, their former dwelling place was set on fire. Roaring flames soared upward in the moonless night as timber, and palm-leaved structures burned intensely, scorching the grassy embankment. As this occurred, a young warrior walked over to where the dead bodies lay. His eyes widened. "Kayapa *is* telling the truth," he yelled. "The woman is not here."

"Maybe, a big cat has dragged her away," was the explanation given by another boy, joining him.

The men rushed back to their leader and repeated their findings.

"Kayapa!" the leader yelled, "Use your *powers;* find the woman!"

The girl gifted with incredible powers *knew* precisely where the missionary was hiding, but something deep inside her big caring heart told her not to reveal this information.

All eyes followed her, heading off into dense forest until she disappeared. Kayapa waited behind a tree for what seemed like ages, and then made her way back to the waiting men. Poker-faced, she announced persuasively, "I did not find the woman, but I did smell the fresh urine of a male jaguar."

"See, I was right!" exclaimed the boy. "A cat did feast this night."

"That solves that problem," the leader said. "Let us return to our women. Then when the sun breaks through, we must return to finish what we must do."

♀

Much earlier, before the reappearance of the torch-carrying men, Belicia Godwin's eyes opened. Dazed, she had no idea how long the "blacking out" spell had lasted. Now, with alert electrical activity in her brain, the past events reran. One minute she saw herself on Amazon territory; there to "educate" the natives, and the next playout, she was face down, with a blow-dart sticking out of her hip. Pain-filled eyes looked about her. She could see them—her beloved husband and her precious sons, lying on the ground. She called out, "Josiah, my boys, can you hear me?"

The silence or signs of movement affected Belicia to cry out hysterically, "Please help me, Jesus, I must get to them!"

Her left leg was in the throes of paralysis from the curare, and refusing to cooperate, but Belicia dragged herself over to where her loved ones lay.

She checked pulses. Not a beat resonated through Belicia's fingers.

Stricken with grief, a sobbing Belicia tenderly closed their eyelids. "I believe I'll be joining you soon, my darlings, as I feel the end of my life approaching as poison flows in my bloodstream…"

She paused to think of her next words. "If our Lord Jesus has other plans for me, and I survive, I'll continue our mission to bring His word to the ungodly. However, if His design isn't to be, I'll see you soon."

The grieving wife and mother kissed her family goodbye, "In this, your traumatic ending of life, may they rest in peace and rise in glory."

Miles away from civilization, and all alone, somewhere deep inside her, Belicia realized she must find the will to survive and get help for her dead family to give them a proper Christian burial.

With iron discipline, the former nurse clenched her teeth against expected suffering, and broke off the top of the bamboo dart. An agonizing cry escaped. Though in acute pain, medical training warned her that attempting to remove the remaining barb from an impaled bone that could cause fatal hemorrhaging.

At this very moment, the grief-stricken and pain-ridden woman didn't care if she died or not.

⊙ʃ၀

There would be no viable reason, or anecdotal evidence, in the modern medical times as to how or why Belicia Analena Godwin didn't instantly perish, like her family, to the deadly curare poison injected into her by the blow-dart.

Was it because only *one* dart had entered her body and not multiple barbs as had been the case of the dead?

The truth is stranger than fiction!

⊙ʃ၀

Shortly after Belicia had snapped off the upper half the dart, the skies turned to stormy darkness, followed by the ear-splitting claps of thunderbolts. The dark heavens opened its doors, and torrential rainfall bucketed down onto the feverish woman, who was grateful for this moment of respite. While voracious thunderclaps continued pealing, an equally powerful force of intuitive survival poked her psyche. Belicia realized that she should devise a plan if she were to live to see another day. Thoughts spurred her on: *You must look for a safe hiding place for the night. And in the morning light, if still alive, God willing, and with his help, you'll make it to the river's edge and maybe flag down a passing boat.*

Memory gave her a nudge: *Tie your red scarf if you need help.*

In life-saving mode, Belicia bum-shuffled her inflamed body towards a nearby cluster of trees with exposed roots and thick mint-green leaves drooping downward. The injured woman wormed her body into the bole (wide gap) at the base of the two-hundred-year-old tree. Uncomfortably inserted, the only sounds to be heard were heavy rainfall and caroling of plum-throated cotinga birds and other nocturnal creatures high above.

The exhausted, pain-filled missionary blacked out.

What would she have done if she had been awake when Kayapa had popped her head into the bole?

As unconsciousness kept the missionary in another time and place, the Waorani, as planned, returned before sunrise to the area. What happened next would be considered ghoulish in modern days, but not in primitive ways. The "deed" was self-preservation passed down to the Waorani by their ancient ancestors.

The leader cut open the chests of the five dead men and re-moved their bluing hearts. He then placed the hearts (which had beat about 100,000 times per day), in a palm-braided basket—then boiled the organs to mash over a fire. The ghoulish residue was taken deep into the forest for ancestral ritual offering to the sacred tree spirits to protect the jungle natives should further intruders from the outside world invade *their* territory.

Death of the physical body, in their culture, is interpreted seri-ously. The Waorani believed that the human heart *is* the soul or spirit which can invade the brains of living humans. So with their hearts detached from their bodies, the members of a white tribe could not possess their native bodies.

Or so it was believed.

After the barbaric heart dissections and disarticulation of their genitals, vine rope nooses suspended the lifeless bodies of Josiah and his sons from the thick boughs of an ancient tree.

What was their crime?

Just respecting their Christian beliefs, hoping the teachings of Jesus Christ would *change* the hearts and minds of pagans.

Was this thinking a cognitive disorder?

Absolutely!

But then missionaries were taught this religious commitment:

"A man who is full of the love of God is not content with blessing his family only, but thinks about all the people in the world, anxious to bless the whole human race."

This quoted religious fervor was not of much of a consolation to the survivor, Belicia. A part of her wished she'd "passed over" with her beloved family. They had been her everything. And the other part was—This missionary truly believed that God had *spared* her to carry on His teachings, but mostly, to give her family a true Christian burial far away from this godless, immoral land.

Unanswered questions remained silent:

Would their ghosts haunt the Amazon rainforest if she was unsuccessful in removing their mutilated bodies?

Or were they already peacefully residing in the kingdom of their Maker?

Not a snowball's chance in hell!

Chapter Seven

Deep in the Amazon Jungle

- THE DARK OF NIGHTTIME -

"There is telepathy between hearts."
—UNKNOWN

It was after midnight, Saturday 14 of October. Raucous snoring was Kayapa's cue. She rose from the bed of palm leaves shared with her husband, put her sleeping baby in a reed carrier, and stealthily sneaked out of their makeshift home. With speedy strides, she headed along the familiar path away from her slumbering people. Through telepathic communication, the "gifted" girl delivered Belicia message: *I'm coming, white woman. I possess good energy, healing powers. You shall not die this night. Your blood will not feed flies and worms, and your heart will not be an offering to tree spirits. You will not become a shadow being!*

Inexplicably, the girl's subliminal message, an incredulous reality, *was* received by the Belicia, who would become an inadvertent "player" in this game of life and death.

Outside the ancient tree, the hammering of raindrops drumming on tree bark brought Belicia back to Earth. She pinched her arm. Was she dreaming? Had she heard an ethereal voice of an angel? It took only seconds to realize that she was still alive. She bowed her head and uttered a silent prayer: *Thank you, Jesus. You have, indeed, spared my life. For what purpose I do not know at this time, but whatever you have planned, I will obey. And I will feel no pain thanks to your loving compassion.*

Belicia's body stiffened as she heard the snapping of broken twigs. She put a hand over her mouth to stifle an imminent scream. *Could it be a hungry jungle creature ready for a meal? Was it the Waorani butchers returning to end her life?*

Panicked, she tried pushing herself further into the bole, but to her dismay, her rotund stature refused to cooperate. The internal dialogue had its say: *This is not happening, woman, unless your fat body shrinks to the size of a walnut.* If it hadn't been a horrible situation, Belicia would have laughed at her silliness.

She fearfully awaited her fate.

Not far away, Kayapa sensed the missionary's anxiety and hurried.

The Waorani girl reached the tree base and jutted her head inside, saying softly, "Do not be afraid. It's me, Kayapa, the one who did not tell of your hiding place. I've come to help you."
Even though Belicia didn't understand, she felt unthreatened. The soft-tone of that young female voice was calming to jangled nerves. Slowly, Belicia inched her way out of the bole to meet the shadowy silhouette. Unsure if Kayapa would understand the Spanish lan-

guage, Belicia placed her hand on her chest to introduce herself, "My name is Belicia."

Kayapa needed no translation. "I'm Kayapa, healing spirit of many tongued spirits. I understand you. You must lie down so I can make your wound well."

Belicia was amazed by how well the girl conversed in Spanish. A tinge of regret befell her. "I should have learned at least some of your language before traveling to the Amazon."

Kayapa smiled, displaying misaligned, uneven teeth and wordlessly gestured to a thick mound of fallen leaves for Belicia to lie down.

Under bright starlight, the spiritual healer kneeled beside Belicia. With her hand aglow like burning coals, Kayapa pulled the remaining dart shaft with the metal barb out of the survivor's hip as if it was no more than a wasp's sting. No cries of pain came from Belicia's lips. No injury swelling or a drop of blood was visible. It was as if the survivor had not sustained a dart wound. However, the missionary was "uncomfortable" with the likelihood Kayapa had supernatural powers beyond balanced imagination. But this girl *had* saved her, and gratitude abounded, "Thank you, kind Kayapa, for taking out the barb, but I feel like it is still embedded because my blood is boiling."

"That is because curare still flows in your veins, but I have made sure it does not take your life."

Belicia's silent feelings were now even more disturbing: *Was it the work of Satan, to gain her trust? Was He testing her Christian beliefs?*

Uncertainty was interrupted by wailing. Noticing the basket

wiggling, Belicia queried, "You have a baby? Is it a girl or a boy?"

"A daughter," Kayapa announced. "Her name will not be revealed to me until the full moon rises, then I will know what the sacred spirits have chosen for her."

To Belicia, the girl's ability to switch languages at will was remarkable. This discovery brought a long sigh.

Before embarkation of this ill-fated trip, the Mompiche hotel owner, Cosme, had offered Belicia a handbook, containing some of the Amazon tribal languages, and the Waorani's tongue was within its pages.

Oh, how I regret not accepting that book to learn the basics of this language.

Sitting upright in the bed of leaves, Belicia placed her arms in a cradling position. "May I hold the baby?"

Kayapa handed over her wailing child without hesitation.

Humming Belicia softly rocked the infant. "What a precious soul," she said, looking into velvety brown eyes. Belicia addressed Kayapa. "I wish I had time to get to know you and your baby, but I must leave this place to get help for my dead family. Please, can you help me to the river's edge?"

A missionary and a native baby's "bonding" was about to become ominous. It was to end a chapter, but not the end of their story.

Chapter Eight

Mompiche Fishing Village, Ecuador

- SATURDAY, OCTOBER 14 -

"Dear God, let this be just a nightmare."
— Roy Horn

Sometime after midnight, Adelmo's wife bolted upright in bed. She placed her hand firmly on her husband's back, shaking him. "Wake up!" she pleaded at the top of your voice. "You're having a nightmare. You keep yelling, "I'm coming! I'm coming!""

Sleepy eyes snapped open. In short heavy breaths, Adelmo emerged from his nightmare to reality. "I'm sorry if I woke you from sleep—"

The nightmare flashed. Vivid images played out—dead bodies, a familiar person sobbing, and an Indian female whose haunting disembodied voice had murmured: *I won't let you die this night.*

Guilt encased his being.

Adelmo took hold of his wife's hand and relayed his dream,

then said, "I can't wait a week as I promised them. I must go back now. I believe they've met with horrible deaths. I saw their ending in my dream."

"Shall I come with you?" his wife offered.

"No, it is much too dangerous," he replied protectively. With his conscience troubling him, the boat owner dressed hurriedly.

Hours later, the wooden boat sailed into the river inlet towards the previous drop-off area. The smell of burning embers hit Adelmo's nostrils. He noted the vacant landscape. For sure, they had burned down their homes. His eyes surveyed the area range. There, flapping in a breeze was the red scarf tied to a murumuru tree. But there was no sign of the person to whom the wrap belonged. He called out, "American people, where are you?"

Eerie silence met his ears. Way too quiet for his liking because the forest was always abuzz with parrots squawking and other screeching creatures going about their business. He called out again. "Is anyone here?"

From behind a giant tree, coming toward him, was the wobbly-legged Belicia, supported by the girl in his dream. Adelmo raced towards them. "Are you okay? I don't see your husband and sons."

Tears streamed down Belicia's ashen cheeks. "They are dead, Adelmo. They were killed by the Waorani, this girl's people."

Adelmo swiftly reached for a machete strung at his waist. "Put that away!" Belicia protested. "*She* didn't kill them. Only God knows why she saved me from the same death. She removed the poisonous dart from my body—"

Kayapa put her fingers to her lips to quiet Belicia.

The Waorani girl sensed *they* were watching. Waving her arms in the air as if warding off evil, she implored loudly, "Leave NOW!"

Kayapa pushed Belicia towards Adelmo. "She's right," he said. "I feel something bad is to happen. We must leave NOW!" But Belicia was having none of it. She turned to her lifesaver, begging, "Please, come with us, beautiful, loving girl. I can give you and your child a better life…"

Several darts struck the girl in the back. Curare sped through her veins as, she dropped face down in the river mud.

Belicia and Adelmo froze like Siberian ice. The boat owner felt like he was experiencing his previous dream in slow motion. In an icy grip of terror, Belicia's shrieks reached the heavens. "God, protect us, and save Kayapa!"

"Your prayer is too late for *her*," Adelmo affirmed.

His strong arms propelled by adrenalin, literally hurled Belicia into the hull of his boat. With her body doubled up, she heard Kayapa's last words, "White woman, you must take my baby. Don't leave her here to be sacrificed to the tree spirits."

Tears cascading, Belicia begged Adelmo, "Get the baby!" she ordered, pointing to the reed basket lying alongside the dying mother. "I can't leave the child to die with her mother."

Adelmo gave Belicia: "*No way, Jose*" expression. And Belicia's silent retort to the boat owner was a profound: NO. Aloud, she bribed, "I will pay you well. Get the baby!"

That incentive did it!

Adelmo raced like a wild cat on a kill, snatched up the basket, and hurled the baby carrier into Belicia's waiting arms. She soothed the wailing baby by placing a thumb in its suckling mouth.

"Let's get out of here," a fearful Adelmo uttered.

With Herculean strength, he pushed the boat off the sand-bar and thrust it out into the river. The jungle escapees were not out of the woods.

From out of nowhere, an eerie, thick mist began to encircle the boat. And a fierce wind like, no other Adelmo had known, whipped up waves that threatened to submerge the wooden boat and drown them all. With the high-pitched slapping sound of oars making contact with "dark" waters, Adelmo rowed as if he was in a race, waiting, waiting… for it to happen.

And it did.

The sound of whizzing darts hitting the waters behind the boat was indeed scary. Thankfully none had found their intended targets. It was as if this life and death situation had never enacted out.

Was someone not of this earth safeguarding them? Was it Kayapa? Was it the slain Godwin family? If not, was it divine intervention as Belicia claimed it to be?

◌⟊◌

Five hours later upon entering the Mompiche jetty, Adelmo bellowed to the fishermen tinkering with their boats. "Help me quickly."

In the days that followed, Belicia's survival story would make media headlines.

Would she be caught in the crosshairs of skeptics, many of whom disbelieved her incredible tale of events? The consensus was: What was she hiding?

Chapter Nine

Quito, Ecuador

- OCTOBER 14, 1918 -

*"Nobody can go back and start a new beginning,
but anyone can start today and make a new ending."*
—MARIA ROBINSON

The Mompiche hotel owner, Cosme Fuerza, a retired military aviator, flew his 1910-built aircraft directly toward the capital of Ecuador. Forty-three minutes later, the experienced pilot landed and delivered his passengers to the waiting ambulance. "Get better soon," Cosme wished Belicia. "I wish that one day you can put this terrible experience behind you."

"Thank you, Cosme," she replied. "I will always be grateful to you and Adelmo."

The old military horse-drawn ambulance transported its patients to Mitad del Mundo (Middle of the World), a township on the outskirts of Quito in Ecuador. At the privately-owned hospital in Mitad del Mundo, a parked squad car, hospital staff, and two reporters, a male, and a female, from the daily newspaper were awaiting their arrival. Fresh out of journalism school, a young man was keen to get the exclusive "scoop" of his career, having learned from Cosme that this American woman and a newborn child have survived a massacre. To his chagrin, an armed officer stationed outside the medical building barred his further approach. The reporter wasn't overly concerned because he had an ace up his sleeve. His sister was one of the emergency hospital staff. She would give him the story!

Kayapa's child, wailing her head off, was removed from Belicia's arms and rushed to the neonatal ward by a nurse.

Their separation would later be enforced, kept apart, by those in authority.

The hospital's top emergency physician, Dr. Bolono Pérez, stood by the patient's side in the ER. "Buenos dias, Señora Godwin," the sixty-year-old physician greeted. The ambulance driver had previously informed him that the American patient was fluent in Spanish.

"I've fragments of what has happened to you, but could you tell me in your own words how you came about to be in the Amazon jungle?"

"Buenos dias," Belicia returned. "What I'm about to tell you will probably stupefy your professional mind, but I can assure you I'm mentally sound. I will explain as best I can."

Bolono's stoic facial demeanor indicated otherwise: *I will be the judge of that!*

Her hands clasped tightly, the evangelist relived the horrific events, how she had witnessed her family's demise, and how she had cheated death from a poisonous blow-dart. "God was watching over me," was her conclusion.

Bolono's face had remained unruffled throughout the retelling. To his knowledge, no one had escaped from the clutches of lethal curare without being permanently paralyzed or worse, dead.

Maybe she was the first! Did she experience Divine intervention?

With Belicia's skirt raised to waist level for examination, a perplexed frown furrowed the physician's forehead. It was more than baffling. There was *no* visible entry wound to support her story. The flesh that covered her hip was unblemished. The professional faced a medical puzzle. It was time to voice his thoughts, "Señora Godwin, I find your tale of what happened to you in the Amazon jungle somewhat incredible." Gesturing towards her exposed hip, he continued factually, "It does not indicate an injury."

Belicia looked intently at her hip with equal disbelief. "This can't be happening!" she exclaimed. "I *was* shot, because..."

She took a moment to muster her disturbing thoughts about the mysterious girl who had saved her life, but knew that she could not explain away the vanished injury scar. So she said to the physician, "When the police find my dead husband and sons, they will also find the dead native girl on the beach. I know she won't be able to confirm, but I'm telling the truth. She, with her inherent powers, removed the blow-dart wedged in my hip bone."

Face-to-face contact brought the doctor's forthright reaction. "Señora, I would like to believe you, but professionally I cannot. The jungle heat can play tricks on the mind as well as trauma. I think that you must have imagined your injury—"

A riled Belicia cut him short. "How dare you make me out to

be a liar!" she irately retorted. She turned away from the doctor's probing eyes to reexamine her exposed hip. Her inner voice broke through: *You must have some blood on your skirt from the initial piercing.* She examined bloodless clothing. Similar to the lack of scarring, not a bloodstain was in sight, only the ingrained dirt.

Staring off into space, Belicia tried to collect her baffled thoughts, but nothing could explain the missing wound or lack of bloodstains.

Belicia looked into the doctor's eyes. "I'm just as confounded as you are, but I'm telling the truth about being shot. A Waorani girl, her name is Kayapa, helped me. I have a witness to her existence," she adamantly maintained. "His name is Adelmo, a boat owner of Mompiche fishing village. He is the person who took my family and me to the Amazon jungle, and he was the one who subsequently rescued me."

With the painful memory of her experience revisiting her, how could she ever forget the look in her husband's or sons' eyes that had captured the final moment of their lives, or Kayapa and her baby?

"Doctor, where is Kayapa's baby? Is she here in the hospital? If so, how is she doing?"

He shook his head before responding, "I cannot give out that information."

Belicia slipped into a mind space that did not belong to this world.

Dr. Pérez quietly left the ER. As a father of four sons himself, he wanted to believe his patient, but his training suggested otherwise—she must be delusional.

The general position of Ecuadorian law enforcement was to leave the Amazonian natives, living in the extreme isolation of the jungle, alone. But they were now being pressured to investigate after a hospital nurse betrayed hospital confidentiality to a relative. The headlines in a popular regional newspaper read: *AMERICAN MISSIONARY, BELICIA MEDENA GODWIN, ABDUCTS WAORANI BABY FROM THE AMAZON JUNGLE.*

The next morning, a little past eight o'clock, Chief Detective Edmundo Travasso flashed his badge at Belicia's hospital bedside. He listened without interruption. Although she didn't fit the "mold" of a murderer, her recollection, her description of events, cast doubts as it had done with her attending physician.

"Señora Godwin, your story doesn't make any sense. I conducted an extensive search of the location where you state your dead family hangs from trees," he stated frankly through his tobacco-stained teeth. Travasso exhaled loudly before commenting further on her seemingly outlandish tale. "It's very puzzling, Señora Godwin. We found no evidence of a crime. No dead bodies are hanging from trees. Or evidence that you and your family were even there in the location you claim. In my professional opinion, you are not telling me the truth."

Belicia tried her best to stay calm, but a rush of anger now broke through her stoic mask. Nothing made sense! First, the physician had doubted her, and now, the detective. She let out a long–exasperated exhalation and then gritted her teeth. She wasn't going to let fear dominate her well-educated mind, now screaming out for truthful justification: *Is everyone crazy in this part of the world? Of course, we were there, idiot. I didn't come to Ecuador alone, or travel to the rainforest by myself! I certainly didn't shoot myself! The Indian baby in this hospital didn't appear out of thin air!*

Detective Travasso continued, "Trying to make contact with the Waorani Indians, who live, in extreme isolation, is virtually impossible, not to mention the fact that it is perilous for my officers to venture into the jungle at all."

Angry at this ridiculous interrogation, Belicia wanted to give up trying to get through to this numbskull's mindset, but her cogent brain wouldn't let her. "Have you spoken to Adelmo, the fisherman from Mompiche? He took us to that location where my family died. He knows the exact spot. What about Cosme, the hotel keeper, and the pilot who flew me there? Did Cosme *imagine* an American family staying in his hotel?"

"Adelmo left Mompiche shortly after you were admitted to hospital," Travasso informed her. "I have had no luck contacting the hotel owner."

Belicia's tired mind went haywire. How convenient! Something was ironic in the fact that *two* men had been involved and had mysteriously vanished. They held the truth.

"I have no idea what's going on," Belicia stated honestly, "why these witnesses had the intent to vanish into thin air, but I do know one thing. The whole of Mompiche village saw me and my family get into Adelmo's boat and saw me alone get out of the boat when he brought me back to the jetty. And I didn't fly to Quito on a magical flying carpet!" she flippantly ended.

Detective Travasso glared at her.

A cloud of contention filled the hospital room. The detective's thought was: *What did she do with the bodies?* He had patiently listened to her incredulous story and was convinced that she was guilty.

Belicia was having a hard time coping with all of this and spoke her mind. "Even if I *had* killed my family, I'm a small woman not physically capable of lifting men into trees."

Was the presumption of the innocence before guilt principle unfairly reversed for Belicia Godwin: *Guilty until proven innocent?*

⚜

After Travasso left the room, Belicia's emotions were raw, not having had the time to mourn properly. She cradled her head, thinking about her loved ones. Her family meant the world to her. She broke down in tears, staggered by the detective and the physician's insinuation that she'd lost her mind and had made up the tragic events. However, it was Travasso's cross-examination as to how she'd come into possession of a native child that also came into doubt.

There was little doubt now that Travasso's stolid mind was already made up—*guilty of murder and kidnapping!*

In the quiet of midnight, mingled hopelessness now seeped into Belicia's depleted spirit.

Was she in a living nightmare? Of course, but it was to have a "wait and see" conclusion. Somewhere, somehow, the wrongly accused woman trusted that justice and the truth would eventually reveal itself. For now, the burden of proof remained. It would be an uphill battle of wishful thinking!

⚭

Even though the tabloids sensationalized Belicia's real-life survival story, the murder and disappearance of the Godwin men remained a mystery. The popular theory in the American press was that the couple had marital problems, broke up shortly after they arrived in Ecuador, and Josiah Godwin, taking his sons, had gone into hiding to avoid further communication with Belicia.

Far-fetched though this scenario sounded, it was the widespread consensus.

⚭

The Ecuadorian law-enforcement and the Indian Affairs officials eventually theorized that Belicia Godwin was mentally ill because the witnesses denied the purported events. Why, Adelmo, Cosme, and others chose to throw Belicia under the bus is anyone's guess. Some say they were intimated by the policía to keep their mouths shut. Some say they just didn't wish to be involved.

⚭

In the time that followed, the media had moved on to the discovery of King Tut. The American missionary's incredible story was history for now.

In the time that followed, the media had moved on to the discovery of King Tut. The American missionary's incredible story was history for now.

Belicia was taken into custody and charged with willfully making false statements about the murder of her family, and also accused of kidnapping an indigenous child. The shackled prisoner was escorted from the hospital, wearing a blue hospital gown and, nothing else.

At the local policía station, the Evangelist in unbelieving shock felt as if stark raving lunatics were processing her. "This is ridiculous!" she protested heatedly. "I will answer no more questions. I have a constitutional right to remain silent. I want a lawyer."

In this period of non-existent modern forensic science, advanced crime labs, and Miranda Rights, Belicia Godwin didn't stand a chance.

The sharp-tongued police captain's cold stare went right through her. "You're not in America!" he snapped. "Need I refresh your memory..?"

He paused for a second, "You are in South America. You have no constitutional rights here. You are now subject to Ecuadoran law."

Belicia rolled her eyes upward. The ordinarily mild-mannered woman was at her wit's end. She raged, "Anyone accused of a crime that they didn't commit is entitled to a lawyer, no matter what country they are in."

Chortles of mirth echoed around the small building.

Outside the station, foreign media gathered, frenziedly bombarding the staff coming in and out of the building with questions:

"Did she fake their deaths?"

"Have they been found alive?"

"Did she fake her injuries?"

"Is it true that she stole a Waorani Indian baby?"

"Where is the child?"

"Is she alive or dead?'

The police officers standing guard were unprepared for the next questions posed by a journalism student with a keen investigative mind. She had waited outside the hospital all day, hoping to get an interview with Belicia. But couldn't get anywhere near the new patient. Now, she addressed the uniformed men, "Do you have any actual evidence that she committed the crimes? If she *is* telling the truth, will you apprehend the Waorani Indians to file murder charges? Is your investigation a gross miscarriage of justice against this missionary woman?"

Public opinion was that Belicia was lying—that she *had* murdered her family—and elaborately concocted the most unbelievable story to feign her innocence. However, there were no such reservations in the minds of those who loved her.

The evangelist had a monumental outpouring of sympathy.

Hundreds of loyal church supporters would arrive in the capital of Ecuador in the coming days. One supporter blew her mind.

Belicia wasn't a star-struck person. To her amazement, a movie star, Theda Bara, who featured in the famous movie, Cleopatra, in 1917, sent her best wishes via an American tabloid reporter. To top that, someone who had known Belicia from the day of her birth would lend more than sympathy.

ojo

Wednesday, 18 of October, Belicia, her face dreary with despair that spread across her dark features, was put in a windowless paddy-wagon and transported to Pichincha Women's Prison, outside Quito. Flanked by two burly female guards, Belicia, still in the cotton hospital garb, felt all alone in a time of greatest need. Like dying embers, she presumed her life was over. She tried communicating with her escorts: "Where are you taking me?" A guard with detached emotional coldness responded irritably, "*Silencó!*"

Could this honest, God-fearing evangelist ever escape from the darkness and be able to summon the "light" back into her life?

Perhaps!

ojo

Belicia was unaware of her final destination. She had no knowledge of Pichincha Prison, but would soon come to learn that this overcrowded hardcore jail held hundreds of women, and was notorious for the unfettered practice of inhumane mistreatment, unspeakable abuse of its prisoners.

As the paddy-wagon pulled into the prison gates, Belicia observed the two-story building, with its crumbling grimy stone walls, the paint long since peeled off. Numerous pocket-sized windows with rusty iron bars gazed outwards from the decaying building. Every available space outside the windows hung items of clothing—the drying washing.

Her eyelids closed tight. *Was this real, or just a bad nightmare?*

The metal exterior jail door clanged shut behind the evangelist.

She was escorted into a large bustling courtyard. The noise from her fellow prisoners, going about their daily business, was overwhelmingly loud. Belicia had never seen so many gaunt faces, lifeless eyes full of despair, in a fog of lost hopes and dreams.

Belicia was processed as an American tourist, despite her being of Latina ancestry. But that was the least of concerns. Humiliation waited.

The new inmate was ordered to remove the only item of clothing she was wearing—the hospital gown.

What happened next would leave the modest wife and mother in tears.

Belicia Godwin underwent the degradation of the prison examination, a vaginal, and an anal cavity search. Following this mortification, Belicia entered a small cubicle adjacent to the examination room. The cold shower water washed away the grime off Belicia's body but not the inescapable psychological trauma.

When the shower water turned off, no towel awaited her. But prison garb, a horizontally-striped baggy grey dress clung to wet skin. No underwear or footwear, the new prisoner was marched to the warden's grimy office that reeked of body odor. There, Belicia faced a big-boned, mean-looking female with wide-spaced dark eyes; the right one set noticeably higher than the left. The gnarly woman's long hardened nails looked like switchblades.

"You'll get no preferential treatment here just because you are

The Little Breadwinner

an American," the grating voice stated. "You will obey the prison rules." Her abnormal eyes fixed onto Belicia's. "And you will pay for your prison clothing and meals."

That last statement brought a flashback.

Back in the local police cell, Belicia had been advised not to eat the food in Pichincha. Prepared in unsanitary conditions, the cooks knowingly served maggot-infested rotten meat.

Did the new inmate have a choice? No, she could not survive without food!

"I have no money to buy clothes or food. Everything we owned, including my handbag containing our passports and cash, was left behind in the jungle."

"Tough shit!" was the cold snap. "This isn't a luxury hotel." The warden cynically added, "In my opinion, I do not believe a word of your ridiculous survival story. Who goes into the Amazon jungle, a dangerous world, without a backup plan? That's if you were even there in the first place!"

"I've been wrongly accused. I am innocent," Belicia argued. "You have to believe me. I *did not* murder my husband and children. The Indians killed them. I *did not* kidnap one of their children. Her mother was shot right in front of my eyes."

The warden, who looked as if she could eat Belicia alive, acidly interrupted, "It has not escaped my notice that you are crazy, mad. But it will be up to a court to decide what is real in your head, or not! I hope you will burn in hell, *gringa*."

Her statement had amplified inhumanity a thousandfold in Belicia's mind. Still, inside her violated body, a tender heart spoke in grief: *I lost my husband and children, and I miss them every day.*

- 98 -

Belicia heaved a heavy sigh, passed caring, just given up to FATE! It was beyond the pale of reality.

⊙⅃⊙

Both peaks of the Pichincha, an active volcano, were visible from the prison cell window in the barely lit 6x6 foot room. Why she had not been placed in solitary confinement remained a mystery.

In Ecuador's wet season, heavy rain battered the glass window pane as Belicia, the only foreign inmate, failed to fall deep into comforting sleep. Lying on the cement floor, covered by a thin blanket, Belicia thrashed her arms about, as if defending herself against an invisible enemy. Then a disembodied voice seemed to penetrate the cell walls, "Don't despair, white woman. I'm here to help you. Trust me."

Belicia just shook her head, trying not to let her imagination run wild.

The next morning, Belicia awoke to feel that she was being watched—by whom? She thought that a fatigued brain was playing a trick on her. But the object was no illusion.

There, on the bottom of the blanket, was a hollow stick two meters long. Next to it was glinting steel, a bloodstained dart-barb, sparking bright flashes in sun ray filtering through the rain-streaked window. The bewildered inmate lifted the cold barb, and immediately the flashback put her back in the rainforest. She had felt nothing, no agonizing pain when Kayapa mystically removed it.

There was no logical justification for that supernatural happening.

Belicia lovingly cradled the barb to her chest. Her elated mind threw out reality. "I don't understand how this got here, but now I have all the proof that I need."

Shortly after these thoughts, a guard opened the cell door to escort Belicia to the food hall for breakfast and found her staring at the ceiling, gripping the dart-head. The woman's shrieks shattered the quiet of the morning, bringing several guards rushing to her side.

"She must have smuggled it in," was one explanation.

"Don't be such an idiot! She couldn't have! I searched her on arrival," another guard countered.

With arms pinioned behind her back, Belicia was forced forward, marched to the warden's office, and faced the woman whose face was as red as a beet with fury. "You have violated prison rules," she accused.

"I didn't put it there," her prisoner passively responded.

"Well, it didn't just fly in through the window," was the retort.

"But I know who did. It was the dead spirit, Kayapa."

"And you call yourself a god-fearing Christian woman," the warden mocked. "Do you believe your own lies?"

This paranormal explanation was too much for the tough-as-boot-nails prison officer. "Get her out of my office!" she barked. "She needs to learn that I do not tolerate liars!"

"What are your orders?" the guard inquired.

"Take her to the chamber!"

"What chamber?"

The warden smirked sarcastically. "You'll soon find out."

Flanked by burly guards, who were anything but feminine with hair cropped short, and in male uniforms and military-style boots, Belicia entered the dark underground cell known as *Agujero* (The Hole), barely large enough for a single person. The old metal door was unlocked, and the pungent odor of mildew greeted its guest. Claustrophobic, the missionary pleaded, "In God's name, please pity me. Don't leave me in here."

Peals of amusement from her uncompassionate jailors resonated along the stone stairway leading away from the underground chamber that had housed thousands of wretched souls.

Belicia was terrified as an unknown fate loomed before her.

Left alone, she sat on a high-backed wooden chair, the one item of furniture in the cell. Nearby, a metal bucket reeked of body waste. The incarcerated woman now imagined skeletons gazing coldly at her, with icy breath escaping from what once were their mouths.

Panic now devouring her frightened mind, Belicia prayed aloud, "Dear God in Heaven, why am I being punished for something I didn't do? Please help me, because I don't know how much more of this inhumane torture I can take—"

A scream issued from Belicia's throat when something furry brushed up against her leg. The giant rodent hastily scurried back through the hole. Now, Prisoner 1408 sat rigid in the chair, as the sound of water dripping from the chipped stone ceiling pounded at her sanity like a sledgehammer.

There were no words to describe that turning moment.

Belicia once more beseeched her Maker, for her end to come

swiftly and, take her to Heaven, where her loved ones awaited her.

Could she ever escape this hellhole?

Belicia's woeful sobbing joined the quiet weeping of a small spectral form with flexed hands behind her. Kayapa's earth-bound soul was just as wretched as the Christian woman.

In time, the prisoner's tears dried up. Belicia became haunted as to why God would "allow" these horrible events to happen. Had she not devoted her entire life to Him?

Would there be an alternate ending for this woman whose Christian beliefs were now questionable?

The answer would be revealed—

Chapter Ten

An Unexpected Visitor from the Past

- SATURDAY, OCTOBER 21, 1918 -

"We only part to meet again."
—JOHN GRAY

He kissed Belicia's tear-stained cheek. "My daughter, I came as soon as I learned through the media about your arrest. I have a meeting with Presidente Juan Flores in an hour. I will insist that you are released immediately."

The prisoner was happy to see him. She humbly said, "Father, I thank you. Please believe me. I'm innocent of these accusations."

"I know you well enough," Antonio replied. "I believe your every word, but these *are* serious allegations."

His daughter with dark under-eye circles from the lack of sleep, said, "I never meant to hurt you, but I was in love, and you just didn't seem to understand."

The El Salvadoran Ambassador to America, Antonio Medena,

responded, "That's all in the past. Let us move forward now." This academic man quoted Socrates, "The secret of change is to focus all your energy not on fighting the old, but on building the new. Right?"

"Thank you, father, for this profound adage." Belicia reached for his hands across the table. Clasping them warmly, she said, "I didn't think you would ever speak to me again, or that I would see you again."

"Blood is thicker than water, child, and I've long forgiven you for disobeying me by marrying a non-believer in our faith. Now is there anything you need?"

"Yes, I need some money to buy food and clean clothes."

Antonio didn't let on, but he was disturbed by her ill-kempt appearance—her hair matted into knots, and filthy clothing that looked like it could fall to the floor any minute.

The warden intentionally halted his visit. "Visiting time is over. Please vacate the building immediately."

Antonio didn't like this commanding in-control woman but obeyed. He kissed Belicia goodbye and promised her that he would search for answers, as he never doubted for a moment her account of what truly happened in the rainforest.

⚬

Belicia did not receive one peso from the wad of cash handed over to the warden during his visit.

When the inmate inquired as to where her money was the warden replied, "The money is going toward the food, drinking water and clothing we provided you with."

For the first time in her life, Belicia wanted to thrash the woman within an inch of her life. What good it might do her was another matter.

ᑲᑭ

Antonio Medena looked, much older than his fifty-six years. As a passenger of an old Nash Quad army truck, courtesy of the Ecuadoran government, he sat in profound silence, alone with thoughts, some good and some detrimental from his own past.

Antonio's previous life seemed to be a dream. For a short while, he had been married to Rósa Cristiani, the youngest of six daughters of one of the wealthiest families in El Salvador. Their meeting had been entirely accidental. In a mood of nostalgic musing, Antonio's memory drifted back to preceding years.

In 1876, with half of the population of El Salvador unemployed, Antonio, aged fourteen, was hired without experience as a stable hand by the Cristiani family in Chalchuapa, a plains town ten kilometers outside of Santa Anna Pueblo. It was dreams come true for a desperately poor boy. Eventually, it was his horse-riding skills that had impressed the trainer at the Cristiani Ranch.

Antonio spent long hours grooming, handling, feeding, stall cleaning, and caring for twenty thoroughbred horses. The tenth child born of an impoverished farming family had lived on a meager budget to feed a large family, Antonio entertained every poor person's dream—to be productive. But most of all, the illiterate boy longed for education, something his family could not afford to give *any* of their children. Now that he was earning money, the thought of private school lessons did cross his mind. But the decent, dutiful son handed over his quarterly earnings to his father without fail.

In time, the teen's ability to handle *difficult* horses came to the notice of his boss, Álvaro Cristiani. The banker marveled at the sixteen-year-old Antonio's ability to catch, halter, break and train "green" horses, taming his wild horses and training them as required.

It was well-known that Álvaro seldom had a kind word to say about any of his servants, but *this* boy would be an exception.

One day, Antonio's employer, who rarely made an appearance, entered the stables and strode towards Antonio. "You must be Antonio, right?"

Antonio bowed his head in respect. "How can I be of help to you, Señor Cristiani?"

"The reason I am here is to ask you to give my youngest daughter, Rósa, riding instruction. She has always been very nervous around horses. You see my headstrong daughter is as stubborn as the day is long. Can you believe it? She is the only one out of my family who cannot ride a horse!"

The following day, Rósa Cristiani walked into the stables. Her eyes lit up in wonderment. It wasn't to be Antonio's superb equine abilities that drew Rósa to act like a female dog in heat this day.

Seductively, Rósa flashed her long black eyelashes at her "teacher." To her eyes, Antonio was tall, athletically muscular, intelligent, friendly, and darn cute. He was *hers!* It certainly wasn't love at first sight for Antonio. He fought hard not to show any repugnance. She was the ugliest girl he had seen.

At a little over five feet six, she was overweight, flat-chested, and her face displayed inflamed blemishes of acne, looking like numerous needle punctures. One feature in Rósa's favor was her thick crop of shiny black hair that hung to waist level.

Teaching Rósa how to ride a horse, using the most docile of the mares, wasn't Antonio's only discomfort. He became unnerved by the girl's escalating intimacy. At every available opportunity, she ran her fingers through his hair. If that wasn't awkward enough, the smitten girl brought food hampers with luxury items he could never afford—such as expensive Italian cheeses, smoked ham, black pearl caviar, roasted nuts, and rich chocolates. Her need to impress him left little doubt in Antonio's mind that she had set her sights on him. However, the bright boy was not stupid. He reminded himself that he had the freedom to choose a sweetheart. No, his heart was not to be purchased or bartered for on the open market of the rich. Or so he thought.

Nonetheless, during their time together, Antonio got to know the unappealing girl far removed from being self-conscious about her actual looks. She was very creative, smart, musically talented, and was enrolled in an elite school to become an art teacher. Rósa often brought her twelve-string Spanish guitar to play for him. Also, she went to church regularly, something that Antonio had not done since he began working for her father. Now, he joined the congregation, sitting behind his student.

The "hard-to-get" stablehand finally buckled under to Rósa's tenacity … I will not take NO for an answer!

But their developing relationship was not plain sailing, far from it. But in time Antonio's heart finally accepted the girl who was paying for his education.

Chapter Eleven

Antonio and Rósa

- 1880 -

"Love is the only 'right' reason to tie the knot."
—Anonymous

Two years later, the church service was attended by the elite of Salvadoran dignitaries and the notable persons in the Central American banking world. The six-year-old flower girl (one of Rósa's many nieces) lined the aisle with red rose petals. The wedding between Antonio and Rósa was an over-the-top three-day occasion, to end all rich people's marriages. The ladies in attendance (Rósa's older sisters) wore red; men wore white. The bride was decked out in a designer gown and wore her deceased grandmother's heirlooms: a diamond necklace, tiara, and earrings to match. The eighteen-year-old groom wore a likewise expensive white tuxedo.

The wedding table adorned with gold candelabras, confetti, and a five-tiered cake cost as much as a university education. But missing from this fairy-tale event was Antonio's family. His father had passed away the year before, and his deeply religious mother had refused the invitation convinced her son was not in his right mind. In her culture, those who don't marry for love are considered unlucky. She candidly spoke her mind, "Your father is turning in his grave because he knows you are marrying for the love of money and not a true heart's desire. Money won't buy you happiness, son. Satan has bewitched you for the root of all evil—money."

The "kept" man did not protest. Antonio felt his mother was ungrateful, expecting him to pick up after her and, help her with things. He never seemed to get the "Thank you very much for your help," when she had handed back Rósa's bestowed gifts of clothing, food, and money that bought quality seeds. The old farmhouse had been renovated with an indoor kitchen, no more cooking over coals outside. Also, Antonio had purchased several plots of farming land by which his family made their living.

People who aren't thankful often bite the hand that feeds them.

⚭

"Dearly beloved, we are gathered here this day to witness this man and woman join together in holy matrimony."

Rósa's scarred face, concealed by the heavy make-up foundation beneath her bridal veil, was in a trance: *Was it truly happening? Am I for real marrying Prince Charming?*

Antonio's meanderings were nothing like those of the "Cinderella" Rósa.

Mama, you're right. I'm getting married for the wrong reasons!

My father, if you are watching over me, I'm sorry I let you down, but I don't wish to be miserable for the rest of my life like you were. You went to your grave without leaving a cent to Mama. But I will make this promise to you to take care of her for the rest of her life.

Antonio kissed his bride on the cheek, held her hands, and told her that he loved her.

Were these sentiments genuine?

Yes. Antonio found an overpowering connection to Rósa. On their "joining together" moment, Antonio wished to stay happily together for the rest of their lives.

Rósa Belicia Cristiani Medena was a happy, happy bride.

That celebratory day, looking into the beaming eyes of his partner, Antonio couldn't explain his surging emotions, a profound connection he now felt for someone he had previously found abhorrent.

The couple sailed to the Bahamas, a honeymoon gift from Rósa's father's banking partner. That honeymoon night, a loving personal relationship grew out of intimacy. It was more than just sex. It marked their togetherness, a feeling of comfortability with each other.

The standard wedding vow "Till death do us part" would test their devoted promise.

⚬⚬

One year later, at the end of November, Antonio lost Rósa the day following their daughter's birth. Antonio had remained at Rósa's bedside, sadly watching his wife and the mother of his daughter pass away. He just couldn't make sense of her sudden death. She had maintained a healthy diet and weight throughout the pregnancy. She was well cared for at a private first-class hospital after giving birth. Unexpectedly, the new mother had complained about feeling pressure in her chest the day after birthing.

The subsequent autopsy revealed massive internal bleeding.

As Rósa's body lay in the mortuary, nothing could console the brokenhearted Antonio, not even the presence of his baby daughter, who was, in the care of Rósa's family. He did, however, name her Belicia, Rosa's middle name, and Analena, after his mother, who had passed away from the smallpox virus three months into her daughter-in-law's pregnancy.

But there were to be rockier times ahead for the widower.

⚬

Rósa's vast inherited fortune, from her land-owning grandfather, was bequeathed solely to her husband. Antonio was now able to fulfill his life-long dream. He obtained a college education in four years. Then, he entered San Salvador University, graduating with honors.

Antonio's knowledge of global history, foreign affairs, politics, management, statistics, and humanitarian work did not go unnoticed by an El Salvadoran government official, Gerardo Barrios, who was one of Álvaro's many cousins.

This prominent man, who would later become el Presidente, had briefly been at the wedding celebration. On this occasion, Antonio had not received an introduction to Gerardo Barrios.

Whether Antonio liked it or not, the upper social classes rarely fraternized with poor folk even when they married into money. And, by all accounts, many of these officials and other distinguished guests, who had been present at the wedding, believed Antonio had simply wormed his way into Rósa's lavish lifestyle for selfish personal greed and, nothing more.

Gossip was ripe among the tight-knit elite for some time! *Why else would the handsome peasant, dirt-poor boy marry such an ugly duckling?*

But this unfounded criticism was about to change. Does "*For better or worse,*" have a hidden meaning?

Chapter Twelve

República De El Salvador

- 1894 -

"The right to choose your own path
is a sacred privilege."
—OPRAH WINFREY

At the age of thirty-two, Antonio Medena rose from an uneducated lowly stablehand to being appointed the first official El Salvadoran attaché to take up office in America. Fluent in several languages, his career flourished. From the start of his political career in Washington DC, the doting father brought his daughter, Belicia, with him. The Cristiani family wasn't too happy about Rosa's child being raised in America, but they had no choice but to hand the child over to her legal parent. It was a trying time for the newly-appointed attaché, juggling his official work and raising his child. Overwhelmed by the amount of work assigned to him, the day-to-day child-rearing was relegated to a live-in Salvadoran nanny in her thirties. She often complained of Belicia's rebellious and stubborn behavior. "She doesn't listen to me," the nanny griped.

Just like her mother, Antonio mused.

He had no plans to remarry, but he did have a roving eye. His private secretary, the daughter of an El Salvadoran dignitary, was stunningly beautiful. They shared many things in common. But "the ghost of marriage past" had left him determined not to repeat it. One of his concerns was the potential stepparent role. Perhaps, his love-interest wouldn't care for the disobedient Belicia. Being a single parent did have its drawbacks, resulting in added pressure, stress, and fatigue. His devotion to his work had little time now for a child.

♔

Belicia's spoiled-brat, hyperactive behavior improved as she reached her late teens. She became self-reliant, confident, gentle, sweet, and dutiful. There were times when she felt guilty being "privileged," having access to education that so many of her age back in El Salvador, a third-world country, could only dream of experiencing. She counted herself lucky to have clean drinking water, a reliable supply of food being three healthy meals a day, never having to line up to buy the basic staples. She could go to the refrigerator and quench her thirst with a cold glass of filtered water, and help herself to the well-stocked food supplies when so many in her country of birth were starving. But the brown-eyed beauty had never been comfortable with having bodyguards escort her to school. She did not want this special treatment, simply because her father was well-off, able to buy her things and keep her protected. But "no such thing as too much love" didn't exist in her world. There was no secure attachment to her father since early childhood. He simply hadn't been there and attentive to her needs when growing up. However, being an ambassador's kid broadened her choices in life.

Belicia enrolled in a prestigious nursing school, and at age twenty, she graduated with honors. She began working as a critical-care nurse at a hospital close to the home she shared with her father. The nanny was long gone. Belicia put every waking moment into her profession. Nursing wasn't just a job for Belicia it was a calling, as she now put others before herself. That is until she met *him*.

It was at the George Washington University Hospital she met and fell in love with Josiah Godwin, whom she had known only casually. He was a medical orderly, and ten years her senior. Of course, her sole parent disapproved. Josiah was a *Protestant!*

A paternal mindset poked at this troubled father. His daughter's infatuation with a man ten years older had to end. How? Send her back to El Salvador to the waiting arms of her family? Would this ensure no further contact with Josiah Godwin?

One evening, after a long day's shift at the hospital, Belicia overheard a telephone conversation between her father and grandfather, Álvaro Cristiani. "I'll have her on the plane tomorrow under the pretense that her presence at your second marriage is your wish."

Belicia's grandmother died from consumption two years earlier, and she was flown to Santa Anna to attend the funeral. Now, Belicia's shocked, angry face could have launched cannonballs.

She quietly crept upstairs and packed a bag with only the essentials needed. Then, she snuck out the door while her father was still talking on the telephone. The incensed Belicia sprinted for Josiah's one-bedroom apartment located behind the hospital.

He was more than delighted to see her.

Two days later, the couple moved into Josiah's parents' house.

Shortly afterward, Belicia renounced the Catholic faith to marry Josiah, in a simple ceremony at the local evangelical church. That day, Josiah announced, "You are now one of us. God's gift to the church."

⚬⫯⚬

Belicia's first son was born on the same day that Josiah became pastor of a newly-built church. The new mother was encouraged to play a role in reaching the people around them, with the message of salvation in Jesus. Four years later, with four young children in tow, the Godwin family, traveled from place to place to preach the gospel to non-believers of the Lord. It was Josiah who came up with the plan to take his family and travel the world, beginning with South America and then across Central America, to convert the "lost" souls of indigenous tribes.

"God spoke to me in a dream last night. We are to go to the Amazon rainforest," he had informed his wife.

"Then we must go and do his bidding," Belicia stated, but with a trace of hesitation in her dutiful voice.

In the time to come, it would be a goodwill mission of horrors.

⚭

"Yes, my dear," Josiah agreed. "We must do His bidding."

The thought of perhaps entering her place of birth brought tingles of expectation to Josiah's devoted wife.

Would she see her father and the Cristiani family? Would she be welcomed after all these years?

And the prospect of tasting *pupusas* (thick flatbread made with cornmeal, stuffed with cheese or refried beans), again made her smile with anticipation of a possible trip back home.

⚭

Even in this age of dutiful children, Belicia Analena Godwin never saw or spoke to her father since she had left home.

Would this change in time?

Chapter Thirteen

Pichincha Correctional Facility

- OCTOBER 22, 1918 -

"The price of freedom is death."
—Malcolm X

In the pre-dawn hours, a firm hand grip gripped Belicia's shoulder. Slumped on the high back chair in this house of horrors, the disoriented prisoner's eyes slowly opened. A soft voice uttered, "Señora Godwin, wake up."

In the light of a kerosene lamp, Belicia's puffy eyes squinted at the young corrections officer. "What is it?"

"Come with me," Carmella instructed. She gently helped Belicia who was weakened from hunger and sleep deprivation to her feet.

Backache, from sleeping in the chair, made her whole body convulse with pain. "Where are we going?" Belicia asked in a raspy voice.

"The warden will explain everything to you when we get upstairs," was Carmella's reply.

The warden, who didn't have the warmth to melt butter, was now churning the milk of human kindness. "Señora, I have some new clothes for you," she said, gesturing to the neatly folded garments laid out on a chair next to her desk.

One eyebrow rose higher than the other. *Not real. Wake up! What on God's green earth is going on? Why is this cold, detached phony human so friendly all of a sudden?*

⁖

Belicia Analena Godwin walked over to the waiting arms of her father. The elated former prisoner hugged her dad. She didn't quite know what was going on. "Father, I don't know how you did this, but thank you. Thank you for saving me."

"No need to thank me," Antonio replied in a loving fatherly tone. "Let's go home."

"Yes, father," Belicia readily agreed. "It is time to go home from this nightmare that I wouldn't wish upon anyone—"

Her jaw dropped.

To Belicia's astonishment, she observed a woman in a distinctive habit, holding Kayapa's baby, standing in front of a four-wheeled delivery wagon drawn by two sure-footed native Cirillo horses known for their hardiness. The Sister of the Charity Hospital handed the infant over to Belicia. "God bless you. Please promise that this "lost to the true God" child is to receive baptism," the Ecuadorian nun entreated. Then she walked off down the unlit street behind the prison walls and vanished from sight.

"God be praised," Belicia uttered at the disappearing figure. Was this Kayapa's doing, looking out for her baby?

An ecstatic Belicia faced her father. "How did you manage to save the child as well?"

"No questions, Belicia," Antonio responded firmly.

✿

At his meeting with President Flores, risking his professional position with actions that could have resulted in an instant arrest, Antonio had secured favor with substantial "bribes" handed over to the Ecuadorian government and prison officials. This money exchange had given Belicia her freedom.

Free, yes, but at what consequential price?

Was Antonio Medena just a "bad apple," or only a desperate parent who loved his child unconditionally?

Chapter Fourteen

Central America

- THREE HOURS, FIFTY-FIVE MINUTES LATER -

"Every moment of your life is a second chance."
—RICK PRICE

The private single-engine aircraft, owned by Álvaro Cristiani, landed at San Salvador Airport. This eighty-eight-year-old aircraft owner had been more than willing to aid his son-in-law in times of crisis. There to greet the homecomers were fifteen family members, including a wet nurse. Absent from the family entourage was Álvaro's wife, Belicia's grandmother. She had passed away from kidney failure on the same day that Belicia, her husband, and sons had arrived in Ecuador to bring the word of God to heathens.

A smiling Álvaro was the first to greet Belicia. Her aching muscles and joints from prolonged sitting in the prison's chair and the long wagon ride to the airstrip had been evident in her gait as she disembarked from the plane. "Granddaughter, I'm so happy to see you after all these years!" he enthused. "Rest assured that you and the baby you saved are in good hands now. I won't let you come to any harm."

"I don't know how to thank you for all you have done for me," responded Belicia.

"It has always been my pleasure to help you." Álvaro breathed deeply, with the memory of another person. "I wish your mother was here to see how beautiful you are."

Belicia smiled. She had never known her mother, Rosa, but not a bad word had ever been uttered about his departed wife by her husband. Yes, she longed for her mother to comfort her at this traumatic time.

"Come, my carriage is waiting to take you home," Álvaro ushered.

As the weary traveler walked towards the waiting horse-drawn vehicle, a part of Belicia was happy to return safely from the dreadful Ecuadoran clutches to her country of birth. The other half was desolate.

She still couldn't eradicate the vivid image of her husband and sons' brutal demise from her mind. Nor could she shake off the experience suffered at the hands of the Ecuadoran police. Or forget the incarceration that had been a living hell.

There was no extradition treaty with Ecuador, so she was now free of torment.

Or was she indeed?

∽

On the first night of her arrival at the Cristiani ranch, an exhausted Belicia just couldn't sleep. A persistent cough and a night sweat, drenching her body, kept her awake. She thought nothing of it, and at sunrise, a tired Belicia went to see baby Analena in the annex of the large residence. She found the infant, born the same day that her family had been slaughtered, breastfed by the wet nurse.

"Buenos dias," the nurse greeted.

"Buenos dias," Belicia responded. "How is she doing?"

"She's a hungry little child," the nurse chuckled, handing over the contented-looking baby to its mother. Belicia stared into the monolid (lacing crease on the eyelids), almond-shaped eyes of Kayapa's "gift" to her. The infant's native ethnicity was clear—dark brown skin, round face, narrow bridged nose, high cheekbones, and prominent jawline, with luxuriant coarse black hair crowning her head. "Oh, she is adorable," Belicia cooed. She kissed Analena on the cheek, saying, "I'm going to give you the best life ever, and when you are older, I will tell you about your brave, beautiful mother."

෴

In the time that followed, Kayapa's daughter was not a welcome guest, as Belicia had believed. She overheard her mother's eldest sister comment to a cousin, "There is something fishy about Belicia's story, and I can't put my finger on it. Do you feel, as like I, that she was so empty with her husband and sons leaving her that she stole another woman's child?"

"Her story about their murders, I think, is farfetched," returned the cousin.

"The child must undergo baptism, or she is unwelcome in *this* household," the aunt sharply sniped.

"I'm not sure if Father Juan will be willing to administer holy baptism when the adopting mother is a protestant," the cousin said.

"If she and this native Indian child are to be accepted by all of us, Belicia has no choice but to convert, right?"

Belicia wanted to charge into the room and confront her relatives but thought better of it. Belicia's blood boiled. NO enforced Catholicism on baby Analena Godwin. She was of native blood and could decide, one day, what religion she wanted to embrace, if any.

The high-minded altruist's steadfast choice, not to raise Analena in *their* faith or *hers,* would not go unpunished.

༄

Life went on at the Cristiani ranch, and the absent Antonio Medena kept in touch with his daughter as often as he could. As it had been in Belicia's growing years, his demanding career kept him busy in Washington, D.C. However, telephone conversations made fully aware of the misgivings at the ranch concerning Belicia's rejection of switching religions. Antonio chose not to intervene, even though he believed it was the right thing to do for the child, whose soul, in his opinion, was in danger. In a letter mailed to his daughter, Antonio wrote:

"I'll be coming home in four weeks. I can't wait to see how you and baby Analena are getting on. Love to you both."

ᘒ

A week before her father's proposed visit, Belicia became bedridden with influenza-like symptoms—fever, sore throat, cough, headache, and fatigue. The local cold remedies did little to alleviate her symptoms—persistent cough, sore throat, pain in her chest, chills, and tiredness, rapid weight loss and, inability to keep food down, had intensified. As a nurse, Belicia knew that something was drastically wrong when she spotted flecks of blood in her expectorated mucus.

Álvaro immediately called for his private physician to make a house visit.

Before Rappaport's and Sprague's invention of the new stethoscope, the doctor produced an out-of-date bi-aural instrument and listened to Belicia's heart.

After the medical examination, he announced, "There is nothing wrong with your heart Señora. It may be some form of respiratory infection. I propose that you go to San Salvador Women's Hospital for further investigation."

ᘒ

Ravaged with tuberculosis bacteria, almost certainly introduced by unsanitary conditions of Pichincha prison, Belicia's lungs began to fail. Word of her critical condition found its way to her father, in a sealed diplomatic mail pouch. Upon receiving the tragic news that his daughter was soon to pass, Antonio scrambled to find an aircraft that would fly him to El Salvador.

⚭

The army service airplane landed at San Salvador Airport on November 10, 1918.

At 3:00 p.m., on the day of Belicia's 39 birthday and the ending of World War 1, she passed away, holding her father's hand. With her dying breath, she implored him not to forsake Kayapa's child. Belicia pleaded, "Please, Father, take care of Analena the way I need to be there for her and cannot. Make up for the time that you didn't share with me as a baby. Her mother saved my life, and I want you to save hers for my sake now. Raise her as if she was your flesh and blood."

In silence, Antonio's heartstrings tugged at his conscience, sensing it a daunting task at this stage in his life. "I'll do my best," he pledged, but reservedly.

Belicia had a satisfied look, as her final breath left her body.

Imagine how contented she would have been, knowing that if she had lived five more days, she would have learned of her pardon.

The headlines in a South American newspaper read:

RUBBER TAPPERS/LOGGERS UNEARTH BODIES IN AMAZON RAINFOREST.

The mutilated bodies have been identified as the five American male missionaries, missing since August. The body of an unidentified Indian female was also discovered yesterday by loggers, North West of the Napo River. Belicia Godwin, the wife of Preacher Josiah Godwin, escaped from incarceration at Pichincha Women's prison with the help of foreign outsiders. Her whereabouts are currently unknown.

⚬

The exposure ignited a storm of interest, a haunting reminder of the horrific events the deceased Belicia had experienced firsthand, and the subsequent suffering created by a wrongful investigation.

Would Belicia's darkest days be laid to rest in her grave? Was she indeed now *free* to join her beloved family in Heaven?

⚬

At the private funeral service, Belicia's body was laid to rest beside her mother.

When the funeral-goers departed, Antonio sidled up to the priest, Father Juan, who had conducted the ceremony. "God is cruel!" cried the grieving Antonio. "He has taken my wife and only child. Why has he spared me?"

"Perhaps he has plans for you, my son," the priest replied, placing a comforting hand on Antonio's shoulder. The grieving man shook his head in denial. "Father, I cannot understand why I did not contract her disease. I was with her every day following her return from Quito to El Salvador."

"As I have said, God has other plans for you."

Unresolved in Antonio's mind was the fact that no one in the Cristiani family, the wet nurse, or baby Analena, had been infected with the deadly TB bacteria.

Seeking an explanation was now uppermost in the grieving father's mindset.

Chapter Fifteen

Kayapa's Child, Analena Godwin

- A NEW YEAR, 1919 -

"The purpose of life is to believe,
to hope, and to strive."
—INDIRA GANDHI

Seven days after Belicia's burial, the racially-motivated Cristiani family made it clear to Antonio that they were unwilling to care for a child who was, not of their Catholic blood.

That piteous day, Álvaro drew his son-in-law aside. "Antonio, you have been the best son-in-law a father could want. But with my daughter Rosa long in her grave, and now her daughter Belicia, I must ask you to remove the *Indian* child from my home."

This insensitive racial statement left Antonio speechless. Though the Ambassador could afford a nanny to care for the infant, Antonio glared at the man whom he had respected above all others and found his angry voice. "That's not possible," Antonio insisted. "You know I'm not in a position to take care of an infant in Washington. It was hard enough raising Belicia under my heavy workload. And look how that turned out!"

"Antonio, you either take her, or I'm afraid I must hand her over to the orphanage. None of my family or our friends wishes to raise an Amazonian native child as their own."

His father-in-law's cold, uncaring attitude toward an innocent child turned Antonio's stomach. "And you think yourself a devout Christian man? What a hypocrite!" he stormed, running fingers through his thick hair.

"I am sad that you feel this way," Álvaro retorted, "Analena is unbaptized..."

Antonio cut him short, "I can arrange for that," he promised.

"Baptized or not, it doesn't alter the fact that she is *not* welcome here!" Álvaro fired back.

Antonio's repugnance was overturned by his inner voice reminding him of the reality of his circumstances. He was nearing retirement, and quitting his position wasn't an option. If he bailed out now, he would not receive a decent pension to see him through his later years.

Noting Antonio's facial expression of internal despondency, Álvaro pacified his son-in-law by saying, "Don't worry, so, Antonio, Baby Analena will be well taken care of at the Hogar le la Niña (Home for Children). I've already made contact, and the Sisters are more than happy to welcome her. And rest assured that this child will want for nothing. I have offered to pay a monthly income to the nuns for her upkeep and education."

Were Kayapa and Belicia crying in the Heavens? Would their retribution come from the underworld? Was this possible? Coming events would speak for themselves.

❧

Several members of the Cristiani family died mysteriously from unknown causes, in the time following Antonio and Álvaro's final conversation regarding the fate of the Amazonian child.

Álvaro, a professional horse rider, was bleeding from his eyes and ears as he was pronounced dead after being thrown from a horse on his ranch two weeks after Baby Analena departed for the orphanage.

Was her mother Kayapa avenged? Were the deaths justified for the abandonment of her child? Would Analena inherit her mother's paranormal powers?

Chapter Sixteen

Hogar De La Niños*
Pueblo Santa Anna, El Salvador

- JANUARY 10, 1919 -

"The biggest disease today is not leprosy or tuberculosis, but rather the feeling of being unwanted."
—MOTHER TERESA

This day in January, the five-month-old, "forsaken" Analena Godwin, was administered a mild herbal sedative, and then transferred from the Cristiani ranch, by the family's priest. Riding bareback while clutching the baby to his chest under his poncho, Father Juan was not his usual cheerful self on this sultry day. When he had been "forced" to perform this deed, he had not wanted any involvement in Álvaro's questionable dealings.

But the "root of all evil" had already claimed his soul.

The banker had provided Juan with his church not far from the ranch. And he had supplied several hundred pound bags of

---

*Hogar De La Niños: Home of the Children

beans and sugar, plus reams of material for clothing, medicines, and whatever else the impoverished congregation needed. This generosity had figured dramatically in the priest's decision to carry out orders.

Would this holy man's conscience allow him to sleep at night?

No. Juan would suffer one dark dream after another until he had made reparation for himself and Analena Godwin.

༺ༀ༻

Father Juan exhaled with desolation as he handed over to the orphanage head an envelope containing Álvaro's substantial donation. Then Juan gave the nun Belicia's notebook, in which the hand-written pages documented Analena's *true* Amazon Rainforest roots. "Give this to her as soon as she can read."

The head of the orphanage bobbed her head, agreeingly.

Reliant on charitable donations, Sister María placed the money and notebook in a desk compartment. She had been expecting this child since Álvaro had visited her shortly following his granddaughter's death. The head of the orphanage now had a question for Father Juan, "Has she been baptized in our faith? Señor Cristiani assured me..?"

"No, not yet," Father Juan interrupted. "I will arrange the baptism as soon as possible."

"Father, you of all people should know that I cannot allow entry of an unbaptized child."

Father Juan glared at the nun. "Sister, are you refusing to admit one of God's children? You should be ashamed of yourself."

Sister María bowed her head in humility. "I will put her in the dormitory immediately."

Father Juan left the building with a brooding expression on his wrinkled face. He knew this particular home provided well for their own "race"—Salvadoran children—but how would an un-baptized Amazonian child, with dark Indian skin tone, be treated?

⁙

Across El Salvador, thousands of abandoned children were in overcrowded orphanages. In the future, Analena would count herself very fortunate. Many orphaned children were merely left to roam the streets because there was nowhere else to care for them. These homeless children faced many hardships, horrible abuse, and suffering from a variety of fates. But this alternative arrangement for Analena was not as clear-cut as Cristiani had assured his son-in-law. Antonio Medena had no idea how bad this children's home was. But then, the foreign attaché had not visited his country of birth since his daughter had passed away.

⁙

Back in America, the Amazonian child was just a memory, something Antonio no longer wanted to recall. At times, he struggled with his emotions, mostly guilt over Belicia's death, and what had become of "her" child.

At present, at the overcrowded and poorly-run orphanage, Analena Godwin was left in a tiny crib for most of the day. In time, her legs would not develop normally due to being left for long periods in the constrained conditions. The adage in Proverbs 13:24 "Spare the rod and spoil the child"—discipline is necessary for a good upbringing—was profoundly misapplied in this merciless establishment. Brutal beatings for trivial infractions were daily punishments for the children who didn't conform to their "keepers" strict rules.

♗

A decade later, despite the appalling conditions of neglect, the now baptized Analena was a happy child with a "priceless" smile. Though uneducated, (only the "brightest" of children given primary schooling), Analena had an emotional education far beyond her ten and a half years. She was kindhearted and extremely receptive to the other younger children. Many were the times that she shared her small helping of food with her hungry companions.

Analena's popularity changed. At age thirteen, she became an "outcast"—the target of a new, much older, and physically stronger girl with anger issues. Out of the blue, this girl slapped Analena on the back. "You're as ugly as a roasted pig!" the sixteen-year-old hissed. "Why don't you go back to the Amazon jungle where you belong?"

"I've done nothing to you. Why are you so unkind to me?"

A brief silence intervened while Analena gathered her thoughts. "What do you mean by going back to the jungle?"

The bully smugly responded, "Sister María told me that you are not a *Salvadoreño* like us. I heard her tell Sister Delores that you were kidnapped from the Amazon rainforest. A missionary woman named Belicia Godwin smuggled you into El Salvador. She died when you were a baby, and you ended up here because no one else wanted an Amazon freak."

Analena's head puzzled over this revelation for the longest time. Then the confused child rushed to search out Sister María. Out of breath, she stuttered, "Guadalupe told me that I was born in a jungle, stolen from my real mother. Is it true?"

The nun stared at the child whose anxious expression cried out for answers. Sister María's tight facial skin would have been suited to a wax museum, as she simply stated, "Of course, it's all true! Your so-called benefactor hasn't paid me a single colón (currency named in honor of Christopher Columbus) note for your upkeep, since the day Father Juan brought you here."

At first, the stark reality behind this disclosure wasn't understandable to the youngster. But later, after brooding over it for hours, she burst into tears.

From then on, Analena's effervescent character changed.

❧

During her teenage years, the orphan struggled with many conflicting emotions—being "stolen," so she believed, was probably the worst. Now feeling that she could never be a "Mummy's girl," the extravert chatterbox became psychologically withdrawn. Over time, her "acting out" behavior became noticeable. A dormitory nun complained to her superior, "What are we going to do with this girl? She won't perform her chores or attend mass. She refuses to bathe. And at the slightest provocation, she attacks others."

"Bring her to me," was Sister María's instruction.

The Sister placed her hand over her mouth in shock when Analena was dragged into her office, wriggling, hissing and spitting like a snake. But it wasn't just the twisted behavior that was most alarming. Analena's face was smeared red with the blood, probably from a slaughtered chicken that had been killed earlier for the evening meal. Pierced through the sides of her nose was thin three-inch chicken bone. Sister María crossed herself. "Mother of God," she uttered, "protect us from all from this daughter of Satan."

Convinced that Analena was possessed, Sister María faced her coworker who was firmly grasping the writhing girl's arms. "Go and fetch Father Juan immediately," she instructed. "And lock Analena in the cellar until he arrives."

A couple of hours later, Sister María faced Father Juan. "You must exorcise the demon in HIS name because I will not tolerate this heathen girl's behavior. She has brought evil into our lives."

Had Analena's baptism escaped her memory? The priest had just come from the cellar and saw no "possession" no cause for exorcism, only a child filled with mental anguish.

After listening to María's ramblings about Satan, a potential solution came to mind. "I know a farming couple who are desperate for extra hands. I'm sure they'd be willing to adopt a child."

The Sister heaved a sigh of pent-up release then asked, "How soon can this occur, as I don't wish for evil to remain a day longer under this holy roof?"

"I will go and talk to them, and bring you their answer as soon as I can," said Father Juan.

⚮

The previous month, Father Juan received word that his favorite uncle had died, she returned to his place of birth, Masahaut, a rural farming community on the outskirts of Santa Anna. The relative had requested his presence to conduct the funeral service. It was the dying man's last request. Father Juan met the Lozano family, sharecroppers, shortly after the service. They invited him back to their home for bean tortillas, and a place to sleep for the night. He gladly accepted. During the meal, Consuela Lozano confided in him. "With my older children gone their own ways, we can't cope with the planting anymore."

Father Juan glanced over to where two twin boys were sitting. Consuela caught on. "One of my sons, Patrido, has bad breathing problems. He can only work a few days out of the week. I have prayed every day to God for help. If we don't get some extra hands, we will have to sell the land that has been in my family for nearly one-hundred years." Consuela elaborated further on their insecure financial circumstances, barely subsisting on approximately one U.S. dollar a day.

At the very moment, for some unknown reason, Analena's face flashed into his memory. *Perfect,* he thought, *kill two birds with one stone.*

Chapter Seventeen

Pueblo Masahaut

- OCTOBER 1, 1931, INVIERNO, THE WINTER SEASON* -

"Love is our true destiny. We do not find the meaning of love by ourselves—we find it with another."
—THOMAS MERTON

At sunrise, on the celebration day of "Dia de la Niño" (Children's Day), thirteen-year-old Analena was more than ready to leave the orphanage. She warmly said her goodbyes to her younger orphans.

"I will miss you," said one tearful little girl, her arms hugging Analena's waist.

"Who is going to mend our clothes now?" asked another.

"Who will sing and rock us to sleep when we are scared?" a third child queried.

"There are lots of other older girls who will love you just like I

---

*There are only two seasons in Central America—wet: May to October, and dry: November to April.

did," responded a moist-eyed Analena.

Sister María and other caretakers waited at the exit door to give Analena her sendoff. María, who had made the abandoned girl's life a living hell, now, surprisingly, had sweet warmth in her voice, "God bless you, my child. I hope you will find happiness in your new home."

"Thank you," Analena replied. Deep inside, she wished never again to be in the company of this coldhearted nun. The departing girl hugged the other nuns, who had shown her some human kindness during her stay.

At the base of the stone steps, Father Juan was waiting.

Donned in a tightly-woven Mexican poncho with a sombrero atop his head, appropriate for this rainy season, he was disturbed by Analena's clothing which was inappropriate for the time of year. The donated garment, an outdated 1910 baggy blue sailor outfit, deer-skin footwear, and a bare head, was not something that he could ignore. The priest addressed Sister María, "In God's name, could you not have found something more appropriate for this child to wear?"

She replied in a huff, "Father, *she* chose her clothing..." An offended exhalation slipped through the nun's curled lips before continuing, "I can find her something else to put on if this is so upsetting to you."

"There is no time. We have to go," was the priest's curt reply.

He beckoned Analena to join him. "Come, child, we have a long journey to make." The priest took her hand and led Analena over to a nearby tree. She took one look at the means of transport and protested loudly, "What is this? I don't know how to ride a burro! Why can't we just ride on a bus?"

Father Juan's loud laughter sounded just like the braying of the donkey. "Don't worry. She's as old as the mountains. You will have no trouble riding her."

A doubtful Analena gave the female creature the "evil" eye. Then, her fingers clutched the animal's ear. "I've never ridden a burro before, so please be good to me," she whispered through the fur.

The raucous high-pitched "*hee-hawing*" sounds could have echoed across miles. Analena grinned. So did Father Juan, who had overheard her reproofs.

In his mind, this adorable young girl, with a lovely nature, made his heart sing. She was *indeed* different from the other orphaned children. His heart filled with feelings of compassion and admiration for the Amazon-born child treated inhumanely. Previously, he had been unable to escape the memory of clutching a five-month child to his chest, riding in blustery weather to the orphanage where he had deposited her.

⚭

The unlikely pair, an old priest atop a mule and a five-foot young girl, riding a donkey, began their five-hour journey to reach the pueblo of Masahaut. Periodically, the trip halted, to request food and water for themselves, Analena's old burro and the priest's feisty mule.

Having spent most of her young years indoors, taking care of small children, cleaning the dormitory, washing clothes, and mending garments seven days a week, Analena had no real concept of time. She was accustomed to rising before dawn, then going to bed well after sunset.

Now she was free from the restraints of institution drudgery, and her eyes sparkled with awe at the breathtaking beauty visible in the distance—sights she had never seen.

The mountain range of Cerro el Pital, 8,957 feet high, and the active Santa Anna volcano, known as Llamatepic, were magical to her eyes. All around her, an abundance of tall palms and acacia thorn trees glistened with crystalline rainwater droplets from the unrelenting downpour that had begun at the onset of their journey.

As they traveled onwards, the heavy rainstorm soaked every inch of the undernourished Analena's exposed flesh. She began to shiver uncontrollably. A concerned Father Juan brought his mule to a halt, dismounted, removed his thick-weaved sheep wool poncho, and offered, "Put this on, child."

Analena was momentarily stunned. No one had ever shown her such kindness before. "It is okay, Father. I like being wet," she responded jovially.

Father Juan shrugged. What did he know about the makings of a teenage kid!

He donned his poncho, remounted his mule, and the pair set off once more.

The dismal weather was far away from her mind. She was excited about the prospect of new beginnings even though Juan had said little of her adoptive family. He had mentioned that the Lozano family relied on crops of corn and sugar cane, crops of choice to make a living. And the family was *allowed* to keep a small garden for themselves.

⁊⟍

Shortly after 3:00 p.m., the weary, stiff, sore, and hungry travelers arrived in the village of Masahaut. But to their dismay, floodwaters had cut them off from reaching the farm.

The Río Lempa, a 422 km long river, running from its source between the Sierra Madre and Sierra de Merendón in southern Guatemala, had burst its banks. The ensuing flood had washed away the only access road to properties that lay on the opposite side. Father Juan had forgotten from his childhood years how unsafe this river could be during the rainy season. Many villagers, especially children, had drowned while attempting to cross the raging Lempa River. He, himself, had experienced a close brush with death when he had tried to swim across the swollen river when he was a fearless child. Analena broke the priest's flashback. "What are we to do now?" she asked Father Juan.

"I know another way," he replied but was uncertain if this alternative route still existed.

The travelers dismounted, and the priest tethered the sodden mounts to a nearby conifer tree. He breathed a sigh of relief. It *was* still there.

The old single-width suspension bridge, built from wood, and iron chains that anchor the walkway to adjacent tree trunks, precariously spanned the river.

"Hold onto the back of my poncho," Father Juan instructed

the frozen-faced girl, as he began crossing the swaying bridge one step at a time. Analena sighed with relief when they finally stepped onto wet soil.

She now smiled broadly delighted when several yellow, brown, and dark-blue tipped swallowtail butterflies flittered in a cloud around her head. She giggled merrily as the legs of the creatures tickled her face.

Father Juan smiled. "They like you—" A deep sigh ended his words as the holy man reflected with regretful sadness.

After that hat dreadful "removal" from the ranch, Analena had groggily awakened from the herbal sedative given her. She had smiled lovingly at him, as her baby fingers had clutched his hand.

He could never shake that image imprinted forever.

⚬

Despite this dismal day, Analena was overjoyed. The mystical appearance of a rainbow, its colorful colors twinkling through ebbing dark clouds, arched above. Eyes gleaming, she commented, "Look, God likes us because he has sent a messenger."

Father Juan smiled. "Yes, indeed, God is watching over us, but you especially, child. You are going to have all the happiness that you deserve."

"Is this the pathway between Earth and Heaven," Analena asked.

"Yes, it is," he replied mysteriously. "We should move onward, Analena, before the sun sets."

After a forty-minute walk, with the odor of wet earth rising around them, under a glowing sun, the pair arrived at the modest adobe-style home belonging to Pacho senior and Consuela Lozano and their fifteen-year-old twin boys, Pacho junior and Patrido. Analena noted the windowless house, built from compacted earth, clay, and straw, with round-edge walls and a flat roof. It was a palace compared to the dungeon-like dwelling she had known since infancy.

With Analena at his side, Father Juan rapped on the timber door. A gray-haired woman in her late fifties appeared. Her surprised look spoke volumes. "Oh, I wasn't expecting you until tomorrow."

The priest explained, "We came a day earlier, hoping to get here without crossing the old bridge, but we had to use it anyway."

Consuela stepped aside to allow her visitors' entrance along the narrow passageway. "Come in," she said, adding, "My husband and sons are out in the fields, preparing the ground for planting season. But they will be back when the sun sets."

The living area was dark, lacking sunlight or electricity. (Electricity owned by private companies was available in cities, but not to rural communities.) Telephones and televisions were commodities of the future, which only the rich could afford.

Inside the adobe house, the faint flames of dwindling candles drew attention to the four "*Petate*"—handwoven bedrolls (sleeping mats) cut from palm fronds and lined up in a row against a wall. In the center of the main living area, there stood a crudely-made wooden table and four chairs.

"Please sit," the soft-spoken Consuela said, gesturing to the dining chairs.

Father Juan introduced Analena. "This is the lovely girl I told you about."

The woman, who had birthed only sons, warmly addressed Analena, "I've longed for a daughter, and now you are here. You must be thirsty. I'll go and bring fresh drinking water. We will eat when the men come home."

"Can I help you fetch the water?" Analena offered.

Consuela examined the skinny girl with bowed legs, unsure as to whether she would be able to transport heavy clay water carriers. But two hands were better than one. "If you like, but it is a long walk."

"I don't mind. I could do with stretching my sore legs. I've been sitting on a beast of burden for hours and hours."

Consuela and Father Juan had looks of amusement on their faces.

On the way to the water source, the females chatted, Analena mainly asking questions about this and that. Then after an hour after trekking the steep mountainside, they crested to the aquatic source—a fissure in a large rock, with crystal-clear creek water cascading downward. Nearby, swarms of honey-bees buzzed. "What are those insects?" Analena asked.

Consuela was puzzled. "Have you not seen a bee before?"

"No."

Her answer was strange, but Consuela didn't want to dwell on it at this moment. She had a priority. Now with the clay pots, fastened to rope-braided harnesses, the women walked back to the house.

Around 6:00 p.m. (Central America's sunset time all year

round) the men of the family entered the house. Pacho senior was first to speak, "Welcome to our home. You must be Father Juan." Pacho senior stared at the teen. "And you are…"

Father Juan quickly interjected, "This is Analena Godwin, the girl I told you about."

"That's not a Spanish name, more like an Inglés name," piped Pacho junior. He weighed her up. "Is she a *mulatto*?"

Father Juan noticed Analena's puzzled look, and thought that she probably didn't know that it was the stereotyping of a person born of one white parent and one black parent, which, of course, wasn't the case. However, the priest simply went along with the deception. "Yes. Her Salvadoran mother married a white American missionary, Josiah Godwin. Does that answer your question, boy?"

Pacho junior changed the subject. "I'm hungry, mamá," he said, rubbing his stomach playfully. "I worked hard today."

After the meal of black beans prepared on an outdoor firepit, Consuela invited the priest to spend the night under their roof. "Thank you, but I have two animals tied up at the bridge, and I must return to the city tomorrow at first light. I have a cousin who will put me up for the night." He gestured to Consuela to walk with him away from the family. "There is something I must give you," he said. He retrieved Analena's only possession, Belicia's notebook from beneath his robe belt under the poncho, and passed it to her, saying, "Analena doesn't know of its existence. Could you find someone who knows English to read it to her?"

Consuela immediately replied, "Neither myself nor my husband can read or write, but my boys go to public school two days a week. English is one of the subjects taught." With that said, she slipped the notebook between her ample breasts. They headed back to be greeted by curious faces. Without revealing anything, Consuela announced, "It's time to say goodbye to Father Juan, and fruitfully we will see him again someday."

Tears welling up, Analena clung to the priest that she adored without question. Would she have loved him if she had known the truth?

"I'll miss you, Father. Please come back and see me when you can."

"I will try, child," Father Juan promised in a kindly voice.

It would be a promise that he could never keep. Father Juan died five days after delivering the orphan to the Lozano family. It seems his not such a faithful mule, tired of being a beast of burden decided to fling the priest off a cliff, breaking his neck.

At a later time, all who had known the Amazonian girl discarded like a piece of garbage would die from unexplained maladies. Were angry ethereal beings, still dissatisfied in their domain beyond mortal death? Antonio Medena's and other pitiless players' days are numbered. The clock ticked on remorselessly!

Chapter Eighteen

A New Life

- THAT SAME OCTOBER EVENING IN THE LOZANO RESIDENCE, 1931 -

"Take the first step in faith. You don't have to see the whole staircase; just take the first step."
—Martin Luther King

Following Father Juan's departure, Analena was choked by her tears. She felt like she had lost the only friend she had in the world. But that was not the case. The orphan had *four* new friends.

As night shrouded the residence, Consuela placed a sleeping mat next to the twins' sleeping area on the hard-packed earthen floor. "I hope the boys won't keep you awake because they *pedo* (pass wind) a lot," she stated with a fun-loving grin.

Analena's dark features flushed with embarrassment. Such rude behavior would not have sat well with "prim and proper" nuns! But rude fun was around the corner for the unsuspecting girl.

"Pacho, take Analena and show her where the latrine is."

"Sure." Pacho junior giggled. "I hope this girl doesn't *stink* it out like father!"

Analena's' face flushed red again.

A short distance from the home, the pit latrine, under a rough timber shelter, was 10 feet deep. There was no comparison to the modern toilets in the orphanage, where waste was flushed away with buckets of water. "Do you want me to wait if you need to go?" Pacho junior asked.

"NO!" Analena returned.

Analena squatted then ran back to the residence in pitch-black darkness.

Consuela was washing dishes in a bucket of water outside. "Let me help you," Analena said.

"I'm nearly done, child. Go and get some sleep now because tomorrow is going to be a busy day."

Analena had never had any interaction with boys at the all-girls orphanage, and having to sleep next to them created quite a somewhat uncomfortable feeling. On the other hand, she was content with the first-born, muscular built twin, Pacho junior with jet-black shoulder-length hair. His dark eyes twinkled when he spoke. She thought his smile was heavenly. Analena noted that Patrido, in comparison, was pale-looking and coughed constantly. She made a mental note to look for "special" plants to help him.

At an early age, Analena had acquired herbal medical knowledge that mystified the nuns. It seemed that little Analena knew precisely which plants to pick for the various minor ailments of sick children.

"God moves in mysterious ways," a nun simply said.

"Of course," Sister María responded. "It's the work of Lucifer!"

She had read Belicia's notebook and was convinced that a dark, evil force was at work inside the soul of the Amazon-born native. With not an inch of humanity in the woman's soul, Sister María had been pleased to see Analena leave.

But God's wrath for her cruelty was around the corner.

❦

The next day at 4:00 a.m., Consuela Lozano prepared to cross the river and do the planting. She was the anchor of the family and, always rose well before her family, to make coffee from fire-roasted ground corn, to which toasted crushed peanuts added flavor. The aroma was that of chocolate, a delight that Analena had never tasted before.

While the family climbed from sleeping mats, Analena donned the sack-dress made from cotton material of a sugar bag Consuela had given her. "I'm going to make you some pretty clothes as soon as I can afford to buy decent material."

Analena headed to the pit latrine to get there before Pacho senior. She opened the door, and her nostrils curled in disgust. Pacho junior *hadn't* lied.

The toilet stunk to high heaven!

❦

The Lozano family, caught in a seemingly endless cycle of poverty, welcomed with open arms the new addition to their family. Not only was Analena a hard worker, but so much fun to be around. Pacho announced to his wife, "God has indeed sent us an angel."

At first, for Analena, it was a challenge to bond with her adoptive family. But she was finally in a place where she felt no one could hurt her anymore. Life for the orphan was full of happiness, even though the farming work and fetching drinking water were backbreaking and exhausting feats. She wouldn't have given up *this* life for anything.

Eventually, *love* came into the life of the girl, an overpowering feeling Analena thought that she would never experience.

Pacho junior and Analena became inseparable.

Patrido was not that enthusiastic about his brother's blossoming romance. His twin spent little time with him nowadays. Patrido, however, felt grateful to her, for he had a new lease on life. The shortness of breath that he had suffered since childhood was gone, thanks to Analena's herbal remedies.

Since poverty in rural areas limited all access to modern medicine, Analena rose to the occasion. She gave to those who needed a "miracle" cure, a natural "home" remedy—a daily tea, prepared *"Flor de Azote"* (yucca petals), lemon tree leaves, ground licorice root, and crushed thorns of the acacia tree. However, she was oblivious to the fact that her "gift" of healing had been hereditary passed down from generation to generation. At his time in her life, Analena still didn't know about her "original" roots. The notebook was still well hidden.

Why Consuela had chosen to keep the book a secret was for a personal reason, somewhat selfish. A gut feeling told her that

Belicia's last words would send Analena away in search of the truth. Consuela couldn't let that happen. Analena had become the daughter she had always wanted—to lose her would be like suffering the loss of her bloodline.

One day, during a brief rest time under a shady tree not far from the budding corn plants, Pacho junior grasped Analena's face with both hands, and kissed her, twirling his tongue twice in her mouth. Caught unaware, she reacted by slapping Pacho in the face. Her lips had not ever touched someone else's, but she had to admit that it was a super-sweet moment. "What are you doing?" she asked, with butterflies fluttering in her stomach.

"Ah, you have never been kissed," Pacho junior smiled cheekily. "It's a man's way of showing love, Analena. Get used to it, because I love you. We are going to marry one day."

Analena was speechless. She still felt the memory of his soft lips on hers; however, his smelly breath wasn't so romantic. "Next time before you kiss me, wash your mouth with acacia flowers," she said with a big smile.

Analena, the Amazonian foundling, was love struck. She had waited so long for someone to say "I love you."

Her prayers *were* answered.

Their blossoming romance was a secret, or so the young love-birds thought.

Subsequently, the sound of vomiting at the lavatory didn't bring a concerned frown. Consuela just *knew!*

‿

Pacho junior and Analena were married in a small chapel. Their first child, a son, was born just eight months later. Twin Patrido followed shortly in his brother's footsteps. He married a girl that he had met on the day of his brother's wedding. He relocated to his in-laws', who lived in Tecla, 8 kilometers west of San Salvador, and eventually lost all contact with his family.

In the years that followed, Analena took care of her aging foster parents, until they eventually died a day apart, from unknown causes. But they had lived long enough to see the happiness in their sons' eyes, especially the union between Pacho and Analena. "It is a match made in Heaven," Consuela had commented. "They were just meant to be together."

◦◦◦

Having been together since their early teens Pacho senior, and the love of his life, Consuela, were buried together in love. A few days before Consuela passed, she had told her daughter-in-law, Analena, about the dream, a nightmare that had frightened her. "I *saw* a native-looking short girl, with bamboo piercings sticking out from her face. She told me that if I did not disclose the whereabouts of the notebook I'd hidden from you, she would make my final moments on Earth painful…"

"What notebook?" Analena interrupted.

Consuela lowered her head to avoid Analena's searching eyes. "Father Juan gave it to me the day you arrived here. He said it belonged to the woman who brought you from the Amazon jungle—"

Consuela's voice faded into stunned silence. It was too much for Analena to easily consume. But an internal dialogue couldn't be silenced: *Amazon jungle? What woman? Where is this notebook? Had the bully and Sister María been telling the truth all along?*

Consuela brought Analena back to Earth. "Wait here! I will go and get it." She slipped out of the residence and, retrieved the notebook hidden under some rocks behind the latrine. She handed it to Analena, tearfully saying, "I'm sorry. I should not have kept this from you. It is *rightfully* yours."

"It's all right," Analena soothed, "but I can't read."

"Neither can I, but my son can."

Analena decided not to have Pacho junior read the notebook, and had Consuela replace it under the rocks. "I have a strong feeling that whatever is in the pages will hurt me and possibly my marriage. I have a family of my own now. Do I *need* to know the past?"

Consuela did not respond.

After Consuela's death, Analena began having disconcerting dreams in which *saw* the same short woman that her mother-in-law had described. In one dream vision, the ethereal voice disclosed: I am your real mother. Your "other" mother saved you, took you away to give you a better life…

Analena knew the time had come to open up Pandora's Box.

When Pacho junior returned that evening from working in the fields, Analena handed him the notebook. "Your mother kept this secret. Please read it for me."

Belicia's journal entries had been written in Spanish and not in English, as Father Juan had assumed. Her exposés were very disturbing. Never in Analena's wildest dreams could she have imagined her true beginnings. She tried to picture her mother's features. Did she look like her? But it was her mother's violent death, described in the notebook that kept Analena awake while Pacho junior slept soundly.

Fast-forward the years in Analena's life to 1966 the year of Estrella's birth.

Although content with Pacho and her children, many jigsaw puzzle pieces were missing from Analena's background—like were there any dwarf children born in the Amazon rainforest, or was Estrella just an aberration of nature? They did share some similarities. Like her, Estrella didn't have a hair on her body except, on her head, and carried the same distinctive, dark-pigmented oval blemish on one cheek as did she. But there was an unexplained trait that they did not share. Yes, her last-born child was spiritually "gifted" beyond human imagination. She had indeed had something more than her mortal self. But where had it originated?

The "old soul" in Estrella had an empathic disposition and, a deep connection with people; super-sensitive to their energy. If someone was sad or angry, she felt it. And as young as she was, she knew when someone was lying or not being sincere. And she intuitively knew how to balance light and dark thoughts in "broken" people. Her love of people and animals abounded.

However, little Estrella told no one that night after night vivid, frightening visions visited her. Thankfully, the horrible dreams did not overwhelm her, because a spiritual being was always there to comfort her: "*Do not be afraid, daughter of the jungle. We are fearsome warriors.*"

It was no accident that Kayapa was her spiritual guide.

Currently, on this harvesting day in 1969, Analena yanked out the peanut plant and presented it to her small daughter. "There, now you can pull off the peanuts."

(In El Salvador it was common for children to begin working when they are four to five years old).

"I don't want to," the four-year-old huffed. "I'm too tired."

"Okay, little one," his mother said and carried her daughter to a nearby Ceiba, a tree similar to a Sequoia. "Rest here, my child, and Mamá will take you home when I've finished my row." As Analena began walking back to the harvesting, she heard her daughter talking in an adult tone to the tree in an unfamiliar tongue. It gave Analena the chills.

She brushed off the feeling. It was nothing! That was wishful thinking.

That same night, Estrella whispered in her mother's ear, "My *abuela,* (grandmother) Kayapa, has told me I'm going to be a great warrior when I'm grown up."

Analena brain fired shock waves. She flew out of the adobe house in search of her husband and spotted him, returning from the toilet. Pacho junior looked at her stunned face. "What's the matter?"

Analena repeated word for word Estrella's previous strange statement, which had filled her mind with disquieting thoughts. Pacho's forehead creased. Who or what gave his child this ability was beyond the comprehension of a peasant farmer's account. "Yes, our child is odd," was all he could say. "Should we consult a priest?"

"Absolutely not!" was Analena's adamant retort. She thought that the revelations in Belicia's journal were surreal.

Analena now realized that the link between the dead and the living wasn't severed. Her daughter was living proof.

Chapter Nineteen

The Little Breadwinner

- MASAHAUT, 1977 -

*"Nothing creates a winner quite like earning it,
not just inheriting it."*
—UNKNOWN

Gossip spun out of control in the peasant village of Masahaut (population 1,113). It was mostly spread by her older siblings, who had told friends, who, in turn, told their parents, who subsequently told their relatives.

Curiosity is a powerful driving force. The curious came in droves to see the little person thought to have special powers, supposedly given to her by the Almighty.

Estrella became known as *"El Sabadora,"* —The Healer.

The eleven-year-old seemingly cured many types of sickness by just a gentle touch on a patient's head. This "caress," she informed the sick, was to release the harmful "trapped" energy pathways so that she could restore the spirit and body into a proper balance.

To treat some physical maladies, she placed hot stones that had been baking in the sun, on their abdomens. But it was for her supernatural capabilities that poor folk came to have their palms read. They paid meager cinco centavos (about five cents) to have their "fortunes" told. But Estrella *knew* who could afford to pay more, such as the upper-class, and these she charged eight *colones* (about one US dollar.)

Very much in demand, this tiny child was no longer scorned, laughed at, or ridiculed. She was now in need by many seeking answers, but not those who claimed her to be a sorcerer or, Satan's helper.

In the olden days, she would hang under the Witches Act.

Occasionally Estrella would clasp objects such as religious artifacts and personal items like jewelry when recent happenings associated with the objects would reveal themselves. She could *see* past, present, and future events that she could have no *natural* knowledge.

During these clairvoyant sessions, Estrella was asked all manner of "need-to-know" questions:

"Am I going to die poor?"

"Will we have a good crop this year?"

"Will my daughters find good husbands?"

"Does my husband have a mistress?"

"Will I bear more children?"

"How many years do I have left?"

The list was endless.

All of this came naturally to Estrella, something she wanted to do—heal the sick—and ease troubled minds. But she refused to treat those who possessed negative energy. She said that her grandmother, her spirit guide, wouldn't allow her to interact with the dark ones living inside them. And many angry souls, with hatred in their hearts, were turned away. It didn't take long for the Roman Catholic Church to learn of *El Sabadora*. These clerics instantly denounced Estrella's healing, declaring her a sorcerer and devil-worshipper, but there was someone in their upper circle who believed otherwise.

However, all was not well with this charismatic believer.

Óscar Arnulfo Romero was diagnosed with obsessive-compulsive personality disorder in 1966, the year of Estrella's birth. Ashamed and embarrassed by his condition, the newly elected archbishop secretly made his way to Pueblo Masahaut, dressed in a collarless shirt, cotton pants, and leather belt. A wide-brimmed floppy straw hat obscured his facial features.

His conscience troubled him along the way—would there be consequences from this impromptu action? Didn't Christian teachings discourage attempting to discover the future through fortunetelling? The phenomena of clairvoyance, or attempt to control the future, violated the First Commandment: "Whoever sacrifices to any god, except the Lord alone, shall be doomed."

Óscar had tried to combat his debilitating disorder, which was affecting his quality of life. But the vicious cycle of OCD worsened, especially the fear of contamination, which led to the excessive cleansing of his hands, rendering them sore and chapped. Because of this compulsive behavior, Óscar's unsettled thoughts and fears led him to perform other repetitive actions, such as repeating a prayer, word, or phrase. It caused him significant distress. Mainly, his anxious thoughts were about his ability to discharge his higher station of responsibly.

But, now, here he was, standing in line, waiting for Estrella's "miracle" cures.

Óscar's disguise didn't deceive the gifted old soul in a young body. Estrella smiled. "Monseñor, it is an honor to meet you."

"The pleasure is mine, but how did you know…"

Óscar cut his words short, giving pause to his thought: *Silly man, she is gifted beyond any rational reasoning.*

Estrella stroked the man's hand. "I'm sorry to tell you that I cannot cure your abnormal need for control, order, and neatness. Your desire to achieve perfection will not be realized in this life-time. You will never be calm, or have peace in your heart because you have the *factor geñetico* (genetic factor) blood passed to you by your father, Santos. You do not know of this, but your father passed away a miserable man because of this disorder. But I *can* heal the skin condition on your hands—"

Estrella's mouth hurriedly closed. This holy man's foretold portent had been *disclosed* to her. Tears welled up for the sweet man sitting on the ground beside her. She felt it was not something she could keep from him. She revealed his prophesied demise.

Óscar lowered his head. He, too, had sensed that his mortal life would not be long on this Earth. Estrella read his thoughts. "Beseech higher powers for intervention, because in three years, you will *not* die like your father." She took hold of Óscar's scabby hands. "You will depart a martyr, and will always be remembered as the holy man who spoke up for his people when they wept. El Papa (The Pope) will declare you a saint."

The archbishop's face paled at this firmly stated revelation but did not echo any thoughts on the subject. Without a word, he handed little Estrella two gold coins, a fortune in those days. "Thank you for seeing me, child of God. I have taken your vision to heart. Please come and visit me should you venture to San Salvador."

By a bizarre twist of fate, that Estrella never saw coming, they would meet up again. On this occasion, she would carry remorse for turning away the outspoken, kind man who was the voice of the poor in times of darkness to come.

For the moment, Estrella and the family's impoverished lives did change for the better. This pint-sized girl was now the little breadwinner.

Chapter Twenty

The Municipality of Barrios

- 1980-1989 -

"You cannot reap what you have not sown. How are we going to reap love in our community if we only sow hate?"
— ÓSCAR ROMERO

Óscar Romero was born to Santos and his wife Guadalupe de Jésus Galdámez, on August 15, 1917. He was one of eight children, with siblings—Gustavo, Romulo, Zaida, Gaspar, Mamerto, Arnoldo, and Aminta, who had passed away as an infant.

Little Óscar was a lively boy full of optimism. He attended a government-aided school till third grade and then was home-schooled. His father, who was a postman for the region, instructed him the skills of carpentry since employment for the educated was not necessarily guaranteed at this time. Though he enjoyed wood-working, he was restless. So, at the age of thirteen, Óscar joined a divinity school in San Miguel, and then later undertook higher studies in Theology from San Salvador's seminary in 1937.

Following his father's death of natural causes, Óscar traveled to Rome. There, he enrolled in the "Gregorian University." During the onset of World War II, when many other students returned home due to the growing turmoil in Italy, Óscar remained behind to complete his degree in theology. Before the war ended, he became an ordained priest in Rome. One year later, he was ordered to return home by the bishop of Barrios, San Salvador, and Óscar dutifully obeyed. He packed his meager belongings and set out for his country of birth. At a German border crossing, he was detained for his "suspected" association with the ousted Italian dictator Mussolini. Óscar fervently declared his innocence. Lacking proof, the unfounded accusation was overturned. Óscar was released and free to travel home.

Was the accusation, in fact, correct?

So it was. Óscar's secret relationship with the dictator had been a clandestine affair.

Upon his safe return home, Óscar began his vocation as a priest in Anamorós for a brief period. He eventually settled down in San Miguel.

By 1966, in the year of Estrella's birth, Óscar was appointed Secretary of El Salvador's "Episcopal Conference," and the editor for the archdiocesan weekly *"Orientación."*

This weekly newspaper became known for publishing cases of torture and repression to create more awareness among Salvadoran citizens.

Eventually, the good shepherd, Óscar Romero, was made the fourth archbishop of San Salvador on February 23, 1977. His appointment received mixed responses. He was not popular with some fellow priests, who sided with the Marxists, favoring the economic and political ideology—communism—of the nineteenth century German philosopher Karl Marx. However, many clergymen warmly welcomed him, including Rutilio Grande, a priest known for his philanthropic activities on behalf of the poor. Grande defended the peasant's rights to organize farm cooperatives. This priest testified that the dogs of elite landowners lived better lives, ate good food than that given to the *campesino* children, whose fathers worked the state-owned fields.

Father Rutilio was assassinated by an unknown killer one month after Óscar took up his new post. Upon hearing of Rutilio's death, and that of a seven-year-old boy killed along with him, the newly-appointed archbishop pressed the government to take immediate action, but this fell upon deaf ears.

From that time on, Óscar began broadcasting "criticisms" on the radio every week. His purpose was to support the oppressed, educating them about the violations of their fundamental human rights. These broadcasts left little doubt in the minds of supporters that Romero's liberation theology was of two kinds, the Catholic version, and the Marxist belief.

Óscar openly declared that he supported the Catholic version.

Now determined to put an end to inhumane violations, the devoted archbishop took it upon himself to become the spokesman of those without a voice.

ᘓᒻᘔ

Sunday, March 23, 1980, Óscar faced a meeting of terrified

peasants, who feared death at any given moment. "I will put an end to this," he promised. That afternoon, the archbishop delivered a lengthy radio speech exhorting soldiers to heed God's call and stop killing innocent people, or they'd perish in the fires of Hell. Óscar also publically condemned U.S. President Jimmy Carter for the increased U.S aid to the corrupt government of El Salvador. Óscar bluntly warned President Carter that the terror and killing of his people would become unbridled. Following Óscar's radio speech later that day, his insulting humiliation heated a furnace of retaliation in the narrow minds of some government bureaucrats. In their detrimental thinking, the archbishop's *speech*, one way or another, had to be addressed.

What transpired next was unforgivable.

Monday morning, March 24, Óscar Romero was conducting Mass at a small local chapel. A vehicle halted in front of "La Divina Providencia" Hospital. Dressed in military garb, a sharpshooter exited his truck. He rested his U.S.-manufactured M-14 sniper rifle, equipped with a telescopic optic on the vehicle door. The dispatched of death aimed through the open doors, down the long aisle to where Óscar the archbishop was administering altar bread with these profound words, "We cannot love by hating," he said. "We cannot defend life by killing…"

A single shot rang out.

The bullet struck the sixty-two-year-old archbishop down in mid-sentence. He staggered and fell. Blood pumped from his heart, soaking his cassock, crucifix, ring, and spurted onto the small white discs, the flesh of Christ that had fallen to the marble floor. Óscar's bifocal eyeglasses, spattered with his blood lay broken on the floor beside the motionless body.

This darkest of crimes in El Salvador's unrest, Óscar Arnulfo Romero, had been murdered in cold blood, assassinated by an unknown gunman.

Was this the act of a lone wolf?

Numbed worshippers looked on in silence—*What had just happened? Is this real?* Then reality truly hit home. Hysterical weeping and wailing rose to the arched chapel ceiling.

Was the U.S. official position toward El Salvador wantonly misguided?

Without question!

❧

Romero's funeral ceremony commenced quietly at the Metropolitan Cathedral in the capital of San Salvador. This sorrowful event was attended by over 250,000 worshippers included bishops from England, Ireland, Spain, Canada, Mexico, Brazil, Ecuador, Peru, Venezuela, Honduras, Nicaragua, Guatemala, Panama, Costa Rico, and the United States, accompanied by two-hundred Salvadoran priests. They had entered through the Cathedral's side door.

The country's poor folk had not expected Óscar Romero to take their side and fight for their human rights. Now, thousands of peasants lined the sidewalks. Some of them had transistor radios, listening to the live broadcast event and, hoping that this sad day would be peaceful.

Alas, it would be anything but peaceful!

Absent from the cathedral were the government representatives of El Salvador. The vast majority of the country's citizens believed that their government had been the "orchestrators" of Óscar's murder.

They were not wrong!

With the cathedral packed with subdued mourners, Cardinal Earnest Ahumada of Mexico, the personal delegate of Pope John Paul II praised Romero as a man of peace—

Suddenly, a loud *boom* sounded at the far end of the plaza, followed by gunshots firing into the crowd. The cardinal's plea for the people to remain calm had little effect. Sheer panic took hold, sending screaming people fleeing in all directions. Some terrified people, including Estrella and her mother, fled from the plaza and into the cathedral. They joined other frightened souls who were, huddled under pews, and anywhere else they could, clutching one another and, fearing for their lives. Some prayed silently, some aloud.

Separated from her mother, Analena, in the chaos, Estrella sought protection behind the elevated wooden pulpit, well above the surrounding floor, where Óscar lay dead.

Little did she know that the unconscionable madness was going to get a whole lot worse!

The sound of exploding shells became more frequent, and the cathedral walls shuddered. Outside, shots were fired at grievers running from the plaza. Now everyone was screaming in terror. People fell to the ground dead. Others were bleeding to death from mortal wounds. Many were wounded by flying shrapnel.

The carnage of the mass shootings, almost ritual, that slew innocent lives, tore flesh, splintered bones of human bodies—men, women, and children—was pure evil.

The grim cycle of violence continued that day.

A total of seventeen bombs went off in the city, killing hundreds of innocent people. Pools of blood from mangled bodies were everywhere. The intense pressure of blast waves killed citizens, who happened to be in the wrong place at the wrong time.

One seventy-year-old woman victim had most of her face blown off. She hung on to life by a thread. There were men, women, and children who had lost arms and legs and other body parts.

Only *cowards* kill women, and little children was the public census on this unspeakable day in 1980.

Eventually, the carnage did not.

Stark evidence of the violence was a large number of bullet holes that had pulverized the cathedral's walls. Mourners were assured the ceremony would be peaceful and free of "events," in honor of Archbishop Romero. It was evident that murderers had desecrated everything holy on this day of mourning.

What was more haunting was the "propaganda" radio broadcast, by a government spokesperson following the massacre of human lives. This high-ranking official's version of the entire affair was unbelievable:

"The bloodshed of people who came to the funeral to pay their respect to the beloved humanitarian, and the killing of Óscar Romero, was not the government's doing," D'Aubuisson stated, "but acts of the left-wing FMLN (Marxist revolutionary organization."

Major D'Aubuisson underestimated the survivors.

The barefaced propaganda lies did not deceive most Salvadorans. Without a doubt, citizens suspected the right-wing political leader commonly known as "Chele" or "light-skinned" face to be the culprit of so many deaths.

∞

Born in Santa Tecla, Roberto D'Aubuisson graduated from the military academy in 1963. He was trained in communications at the School of the Americas in 1972, subsequently joining Salvadoran military intelligence. During the civil war, Major D'Aubuisson commanded special troops, mainly right-wing death squads, who brutally tortured and killed thousands of civilians. D'Aubuisson was the suspect and believed to be the principal activist in the assassination of Archbishop Óscar Romero.

Following the Archbishop's death, political leader, Roberto D'Aubuisson, founder of the Nationalist Republican Alliance (ARENA – 1980-1985), addressed the public. "I make this vow to you all to fight against Soviet-sponsored communism and exterminate the "Sandinistas" (guerilla fighters) who were entirely responsible for the murder of Óscar Romero other clergymen, and innocent civilians.

This hard-drinking, chain-smoking man, a U.S. ally incensed the Salvadoran people, hearing this broadcast. The listeners *knew* who was responsible for Romero's death, the deaths of fellow priests like Rutilio Grande, Ernesto Barrera, and Napoleòn Macías, as well as thousands of civilians.

❧

Six weeks after Romero's murder, Major D'Aubuisson and a group of soldiers were arrested at an isolated farm. Weapons and documents were discovered, identifying D'Aubuisson as the leader of the death squads at this residence. Confiscated during the raid was a manifesto of his planned campaign—a *coup d'état*—to depose the Revolutionary Government Junta (JRG) ruling El Salvador.

His arrest provoked right-wing terrorist threats and institutional pressures, eventually leading to D'Aubuisson's return from his Guatemalan exile. In a television documentary, the major denounced the JRG–identified "enemies," assassinated soon after.

The shameless man's opposition to the JRG caused international infamy. He openly declared a need to kill 200,000 to 300,000 people to restore peace to El Salvador.

❧

By February 21, 1992, a month after the civil war ended, Major Roberto D'Aubuisson died at age forty-eight, of esophageal cancer and bleeding ulcers.

Was it poetic justice or divine intervention? Was it the retribution by God for killing apostle priests as a significant majority of Salvadorans believed? Some Salvadorans maintained that the major was their hero who "saved" El Salvador from communism.

BS!

Romero's assassination was to become one of the most notorious unsolved crimes of this war. The American promise to El
Salvador, to bring justice, came to nothing.

Did the powers in Washington know far more information
about the murders of the priests, nuns, and civilians than it admitted?

With no captured shooter, officials claimed a lack of evidence.
To this day, the Archbishop's murder remains unsolved in this
dark chapter in history. Justice can be fickle!

The city of San Salvador was already a violent place. However,
after the archbishop's murder, which caused a city-wide uproar
amongst his followers, who could the citizens appeal to for action?
As far as they could observe, other world powers simply didn't
wish to be involved in the unspeakable atrocities happening in this
third world country. Did these other powers choose to turn a blind
eye? Of course!

From 1978 to 1992, the Salvadoran armed forces fought a war
against the FMLN— (Farbundo Martí National Liberation Front),
an insurgent group opposed to the military-led junta government
of El Salvador, who were being financed by the United States. The
El Salvadoran government had received over one-hundred million

dollars per year. This financial aid enabled them to purchase sixty-three military aircraft, seventy-two helicopters, weapons such as M-16s, and various munitions.

ᏬᏝᎧ

In a country of only 5.5 million, more than 75,000 Salvadorans perished in the civil war. Thousands of others simply "disappeared." One million fled. Millions were left homeless, always on the run from the army. Cadavers clogged streams, and tortured bodies were thrown onto garbage dumps. After the twelve-year war, mass graves littered the landscape.

In this bloodiest century in history, Estrella and her entire family would become victims of brutal repression. And in 1990, Estrella would suffer the worst of humankind's evils.

ᏬᏝᎧ

Before Óscar's assassination, the Lozano family's impoverished circumstances were no more. Young Estrella, always smiling and laughing, was now the *real* breadwinner, bringing in more income than her parents. However, Pacho junior and Analena also earned funds from the sales of their sugarcane, corn, and peanuts crops.

"All dreams come true," was now a realistic aspiration.

Estrella's steady flow of income from her extra-sensory perception and telepathic abilities, now afforded the family with comforts beyond reach until now. They purchased 2.47 acres of farmland, previously owned by the elite, who proved to be non-other than the Cristiani family—Belicia Medena Godwin's grandfather.

Now the Lozano property had electricity and indoor plumbing; a pipe brought in from the mountains that delivered fresh spring water through one faucet was prosperity to the once destitute family. Livestock of dairy cows, chickens, pigs, and workhorses, added to their comfort in stark contrast to their previous impoverished circumstances. A further improvement, a fire pit in the center of the home, served as a cook-fire providing lighting at night when the electricity shut off. Their quota for this much-sought service was three hours per day.

The youngest in this family wasn't interested in these acquired benefits, but content to play with her "toys"—colorful frogs that hopped all over the house. Estrella entertained leopard geckos, harmless snakes, and even the odd scorpion that freaked her mother out. "Are you out of your mind? That dangerous creature can sting you, and even kill you with its venom."

Estrella chuckled, and in cute child's talk responded, "Mama, if "Pepe" (she had names for all her creatures) is going to kill me, I would have been dead a long time ago."

Analena couldn't help but love her "special" daughter. But there was some emptiness in her heart for the two daughters lost to premature death, and for her living older children, who had married and started their own families and relocated to major cities in search of making a better life.

They seldom returned home to visit. But then Analena *wasn't* emotionally alone. She had little Estrella, and her three adopted sons: Aléjo aged fifteen, Amoro aged fourteen, and Ángel aged twelve. Her commitment to them had come out of the blue.

One sunny day, while Analena was harvesting peanuts, a farmworker named Rosalina came running down the field of plant rows towards her. "I need your help!" she wailed. "My husband is dead, shot by the National Guard, accused of being a communist1 He told them that it was untrue; they shot him anyway…"

She paused in the sentence to gather the young who had followed in her wake. Their thin sad faces looked like they hadn't been fed properly for some time.

Pale skin, swollen face, drooped eyelids, and looking tired, Rosalina continued, "I am very ill, Analena, and I worry that if I die, my boys will starve to death. I begged my sister, who lives in San Salvador, to take them in, but she is as poor as I am. Please, Analena, if anything happens to me, take my boys like your own. Don't let them end up in an orphanage."

That heartfelt plea had sent shivers down Analena's spine.

⚬⏀⚬

A week later, the three boys, clutching bundles of clothing, appeared at her door. "Mama died last night," said a tearful Aléjo. "Before she died, she told us to come here."

Analena and Pacho junior welcomed the boys with open arms. And Estrella just loved her three new brothers, and the gift they brought for her—a mixed-breed Chihuahua. Pure happiness flowed from Estrella's heart.

Although the boys had already named the pet, Estrella renamed the dog "Cerdito" (Piggy). From then on, this miniature dog and the little girl became joined at the hip. Estrella refused to attend Sunday Mass without him tucked into a cloth carrier bag.

But it wasn't the large-eared pet that irked the parish priest.

One Sunday, Father Gonzales pulled Pacho aside. "You, your wife, and three sons are welcome in God's house, but not Estrella. Many parishioners have expressed their concerns to me about this child's idolatry (worship of false gods), saying that she is a sorcerer. Their fears reached the bishop. In a liturgical letter, he has strongly proposed that Estrella requires exorcism to return to God's house."

Pacho's jaw dropped.

Trying to understand what was going on in these church folk's minds, hearts, and emotions, was quite beyond this astonished father. Without saying a word to the priest, Pacho lifted Estrella into his arms, turned to his wife and three foster sons. "We are leaving!" he irately instructed. "I no longer believe in a *just* God."

Pacho and Analena Lozano declined to enter any church again.

Estrella had no appreciation for what had happened between her father and the priest but was happy not to spend hours kneeling on crooked knees.

She would enter a house of God again, but willingly.

ᖰᖷ

In March of 1980, Analena announced, "I'm going to take the bus to the city, and I would like you to come with me, Estrella."

"Why, what's the special occasion?" she queried.

"I want to attend Mass," her mother replied.

Estrella pulled a face. "But you haven't gone to church in a long while. Why would you want to travel to the city when you can go to Mass here in the Pueblo? Will my father and my brothers be joining us?"

"No, they have to work the fields, Estrella."

Analena puffed out her cheeks. Estrella knew when to stop asking questions. "Okay, I will join you, but only this once. I don't know why, but going into a church gives me the creeps."

The decision to join her mother would haunt the non-believer for the rest of her life.

◦◦◦

While they had been "saved" from the deadly bullets and bombs, there were family members who had not been so fortunate. Pacho's twin, Patrido, his pregnant wife, baby son, and Estrella's older siblings had not escaped the carnage. They had been blown to pieces by the bombings.

Upon learning of her children's deaths, Analena's overwhelming grief sent her into a tunnel of madness. Pacho senior noted her dark mood swings and simply put it down to despair. Even her Amazonian ethereal mother, Kayapa, could not save her from a mental breakdown.

Before the dawning of a new day in the wet season, Analena slipped out of the adobe. When she didn't return at breakfast time, the rest of her family was not overly concerned. Analena often left very early to catch bottom-feeder fish when the river was high. But when she failed to return at breakfast time, her worried husband went out in search. Analena was nowhere in sight.

Where was she? Had she run away from her marriage? No! She would never have left Estrella behind!

◦¦◦

Analena's lifeless naked body finally washed up, after the flood had receded. Was it accidental? Had she fallen into the raging waters while fishing?

Had she left the house naked? Or had her attire simply been washed out of sight?

Analena's death was a mystery for the time being—until a neighboring farmer's wife revealed the probable cause. "Your wife told me that she could not go on living. She wanted to join her children in Heaven. I didn't think much of it at the time. I'm so sorry for your loss."

Pacho's grief was immeasurable. It was bad enough that his twin brother, Patrido, and his children had died in the bombings. Analena's suicide was the icing on the cake.

The desolate man took his grief out on Estrella. "You are supposed to be a spiritual *messenger* ordained by God! Why could you not have foretold the death of your mother, or Patrido, your uncle, or your sisters, nephews, and nieces? Father Gonzales was right not to let you into the church!" Pacho ranted. "You *are* a sorcerer!"

Her father's hurtful words tore a big hole in Estrella's heart, but she knew that nothing she could say, or do, could heal him. He, like her mother, was beyond reach.

No spiritual warning from the past or the present could ward off what fatefully lay ahead for the remaining Lozano family.

❦

Pacho Lozano disappeared from Estrella and fostered brothers' lives the day after his wife was denied Catholic burial. Addressing the act of suicide Father Gonzales stated, "While I understand your wife was not fully right in her mind and thus not one hundred-percent morally culpable, taking one's life is still a sin against God. Analena will not be properly blessed. I'm sorry, but she cannot lie in consecrated ground."

"There is NO *just* God!" Pacho spat.

The pastor of the Pentecostal Church stepped up to help the grieving man. Analena Lozano was laid to rest in his church's cemetery. That same day, Pacho voiced his dark feeling to the Pentecostal clergyman, "I cannot live anymore with such a burden of sorrow. My parents are gone, and my twin brother is no more. My beautiful wife has departed. I just cannot live without her. She was my life. I will kill myself."

"Please don't say that," the pastor said. "Think of your daughter and the boys you lovingly took to heart."

Did the hurting husband and father act on his grief-stricken words?

To the present day, Pacho Lozano has not been found, dead or alive.

❦

Estrella had known loving relatives and biological siblings. They were now all gone. All she had left were her foster brothers. She adored them.

After her father's mysterious disappearance, she made a vow—to keep the boys from harm and never to reveal the destinies of others again. She told herself: "I am done with the "hollowness" of the supernatural realm."

Or so she thought!

Chapter Twenty-One

Lozano Farm

- SUMMER, THE DRY SEASON, APRIL 1990 -

*"Compelled to become instruments of war, to kill and
be killed, child soldiers are forced to give violent
expression to hatreds of adults."*
—Oiara Otunnu

Ten years into the war, the now thirty-four-year-old Estrella was
"mother" to the three young men, whom she loved and made
comfortable around her. The brothers were her life. But it wasn't
easy, trying to make ends meet with extra mouths to feed. She had
given thought about returning to her former profession as El Sabadora, but this wartime bleakness meant hard times for everyone.
Money was tight. But mainly, she recalled making a promise to
herself—no more paranormal involvement.

Estrella and her brothers continued to plant peanuts and sugar
cane to survive. But how long could she keep up, with the market
prices being so low? She was paid peanuts for the 100 lbs. bags.
Her desire to care for and protect her family was a fundamental

objective. She was shortly about to be tested!

Estrella spotted *them*. Her dark features lost color. She wanted to run for safety, but her frozen feet prevented escape. Rigid as a stone statue, she blamed herself: *If only I hadn't—*

Earlier that same day, Estrella trekked up to the old drinking water source in the mountain rock for some alone time to think things over. She wanted to gather her thoughts about taking the unshelled peanut crop and dairy milk to the bustling market streets of Santa Anna, where long rows of vendors offered their products. Many of those in these war-torn circumstances sold well below market value, just to make a dime. Estrella's wish was to one day cast off the shackles of poverty by returning to her unique "gifts," but for now, she would eke out a living selling her crops.

In the solace of the mountain spring, she was just about to refresh her face in the flowing waters when an ominous feeling crept over her. An inner voice of reason advised: *Return home and fast. Something's very wrong!*

Shoeless feet sprinted downward, like a mountain goat, just in time to witness two uniformed soldiers heading for the adobe doorway. An icy wave of panic engulfed her being. Estrella knew *why* they were there. It was every mother's nightmare.

⚸

Before the civil war broke out, no compulsory enlistment. No forced military service. But many poor Salvadoran men were drawn into an army career to feed their families. But it was their children who couldn't be protected. The army came looking for them as soon as they had turned twelve. In fear of this happening, families in cities sent their young boys to stay with relatives in rural regions, thinking that they would be safe.

Not true!

The kidnapping of teenaged boys from rural areas and forcing them into military service was increasing at this time. Schoolyards everywhere were no exception.

Soldiers marched into the schools and, called out the names marked on the birth records. Once the "listed" assembled, they were carted away in trucks, to military barracks, and trained on how to use the specially modified M-16's, as army regulation weapons were too large for these small and reluctant "soldiers."

Many of these children became victims of war and were never seen alive again.

Following the roundups, distraught parents converged upon the army headquarters only to be dispersed by a volley of shots fired into the air. Some upper-class kinfolk, who had the financial means, handed their sons to "coyotes," who pledged to smuggle them into the United States, where relatives would be waiting. Impoverished folks sacrificed everything they had and, sold all, to satisfy to the money-grabbing human smugglers.

Frightened boys girls, and others, wishing to flee from the "killing fields," risked their lives, perched atop "La Bestia" (The Beast), northbound freight trains that thundered through El Salvador, across Mexico, to the U.S. border. Runaways were robbed, assaulted, and raped by thugs controlling the train stops. A large number of the "riders" fell asleep and, tumbled down, where they lost limbs, or perished under the train wheels. Some, who made it to U.S. soil, were caught and detained by U.S. border security. They were denied entry and sent back home to face the "original" enemy that had caused their flight in the first place.

⚜

At present, the abduction rumor of young boys had spread, and Estrella became worried that the National Guard would come to take her brothers while absent from the house. She had never let the boys out of sight until this day.

Now, the overprotective mother's instinct rose in fear.

In an altered state of consciousness, Estrella reached out into the invisible world, "La Mancha Mama, the sacred spirit of Kayapa's jungle home, I beg you, make me invisible, and hide me from human eyes so I can murder these sons of bitches."

Impatiently, she looked downward at visible bare feet. It seemed the sacred tree spirit was occupied elsewhere. Where was the out of this world warrior, Kayapa?

Her crooked limbs fearfully shaking Estrella advanced toward the soldiers. With steel-cold eyes, Army Private Olivares taunted. "And what do we have *here!* I do believe I see an ugly midget! I never *had* one!"

This predator, of the worst kind, began unzipping his trousers.

His fellow soldier laughingly encouraged, "Go for it, Olivares."

The surname of *this* soldier would become tantamount in future times to come. But today, Estrella wished that the earth would swallow her up. Not far away, her brothers felt her terror. "Leave her alone!" Ángel yelled.

The cold hard steel of an M-16 smashed against his head. "Do you have a death wish?" Molino Moreno, the mid-ranking soldier, with the full face of a boxer, threatened.

At gunpoint, he held the young men at bay, while Olivares pinned Estrella to the ground. Something inside her snapped, and power shifted. Gritty survival instinct kicked in as she fought for her life.

The courageous dwarf's foot slammed into Olivares' exposed genitals. He doubled up, spitting out a profanity, "*Hôr!*" (Whore)

Moreno dashed to his comrade's aide, but courage was still at play. Estrella's fingernails gouged jagged gashes on the soldier's cheek. "Bitch," Moreno shrieked in crazed rage. He raised the barrel of his weapon, and hard steel smashed into Estrella's head, sucking oxygen from her brain. The sound of agony in her crying voice was heartbreaking, "Kayapa, bring me swift death."

Detained against her will, Estrella cried out repeatedly, "Please, stop… stop."
Sadistic laughter answered for pleas. The little person wanted it all to go away. That was not likely to happen. But futuristic insight advised her to examine the features of the evil man violating her.

Estrella would not forget *his* face or that of the other soldier. At this time, the imprints stored in her hippocampus would serve her well one day.

෴

Olivares continued to violate his victim.

While this was happening, she couldn't bring herself to look to where her brothers were held at bay. The deadly M-16 directed at them by Moreno, Aléjo, Amoro, Ángel, were so in shock their bodies froze. Helplessly, they watched their only remaining "parent" sadistically raped.

Then, the men switched places. Moreno took his "turn." This further invasion tore Estrella from her body and gutted her soul.

Her brothers were powerless to prevent the sickening continuation of the sexual violation of their family members. Not unless they accepted death themselves, or worse, they could also suffer rape. They had heard rumors in the public school they attended, about *boys* violated by inebriated soldiers. Were they next?

Tears continued to flow as they looked on helplessly.

When the assault ended, Estrella wanted to die like her mother, but silent thoughts intervened: *You have to live for the boys. They will need you when the war is over.*

With excruciating pain intensifying, Estrella's rapists ransacked the house, removing anything of value. Olivares walked over to the army vehicle, removed a jug of gasoline, flung the liquid through the door, and set the adobe home on fire.

Estrella watched as everything she owned, including Belicia's notebook, birth-certificates, and other legal documents, were consumed by the flames, incinerating the chapters from the past—forever lost in time—the connection to where Analena's bloodline first began was in ashes.

While flames soared, the dairy cow was shot dead. Then Olivares tried to grab hold of Cerdito, but the spunky Chihuahua put up a brave fight. Sharp incisors sunk into the soldier's hand. Pupils glowing red in demonic possession, Olivares spat, *"Bastardo!"*

Two bullets fired into Estrella's small companion's head, ending the life of a loved pet.

Artery veins throbbing in his neck and seething with unadulterated rage, Olivares strode over to Estrella, who was curled in a fetal position. She felt the cold barrel of 9mm handgun press against her right temple. An evil smirk creasing his face, the heartless soldier fired a shot at close range into her head. Estrella's body jerked and then went still.

The little person's dream of finding a husband to match her tiny stature and, living happily ever after disintegrated into oblivion. In the background, the "enlisted" captives were heard weeping wretchedly as they walked at gunpoint into the vehicle with their hands tied behind their backs. The army vehicle sped down the road like a bat out of hell.

ॐ

Their stigma and shame remained a powerful constraint to the abducted men and boys, survivors who had experienced sexual violation during wartime. The total count of young boys seized during this despicable war remains unconfirmed.

(It is historically documented, correctly or not, that 921 children went missing.)

When the war ended in the coming year of 1992, unmarked graves macabrely sprung up, like unwanted weeds after a rainstorm. Like most other crimes committed during the war, the soldiers of the National Guard, who were ordered to steal the children, have not been brought to justice for their unspeakable actions against humanity. The perpetrators simply resumed their lives, as if nothing had ever happened. But did they sleep well?

There was a person whose "sleep" would be unaffected.

Loco, a son of one of the rapists, would in time learn of his father's crime that had taken place in the rural area of Masahaut in the 1990s.

Would it even trouble Loco's psyche? Highly unlikely!

This bad seed would follow his father's heinous footsteps in time to come. The apple doesn't fall far from the tree!

Chapter Twenty-Two

San Pedro Hospital

- FOLLOWING THE SEXUAL VIOLATION -

"Dynamite comes in small packages."
—UNKNOWN

Who was watching over this little person was an enigma. Because, incredibly, Estrella was still alive!

Suffering from severe injuries to her private parts, her face covered with bruises and lacerations, with a bullet lodged somewhere in her head, she regained consciousness. She looked around. All was quiet except for the noise of billowing flames. Half-clothed, with hands and knees firmly on the ground, Estrella crawled away from the crime scene.

Swooning in and out of consciousness, she crawled towards the river bridge. As she was moving at a snail's pace across the old rickety bridge, a horrified voice lifted to the sky, *"Oh, Querido Dios en el Cielo!"* (Oh, dear God in the heavens..!)

"Help me... help me," sobbed the profusely bleeding Estrella.

Nothing could have prepared the parish priest, Father Gonzales, for the chance encounter. As it happens, he was the same individual who had instructed Estrella's father to have her exorcised.

Gonzales lifted the barely-alive Estrella into his arms and tears of compassion streaming down his cheeks, the priest dashed from the river crossway, yelling for help. Hearing his cries, a field worker ran to the priest's side—"Madre mia," the man exhaled in horror. "I know her. She is my neighbor. Bring her into my home."

Writhing in pain, Estrella lay in the neighbor's house, while Father Gonzales went off to get help. Foremost in the priest's mind was a grave concern: Could he get her to a hospital, miles away, in time?

Fortunately, he found a willing helper, a delivery man with his transport.

At San Pedro hospital, in Masahaut, Estrella was rushed into the ER, looking like she had been in a high-speed head-on collision. Her blood pressure was dangerously low, putting her at high risk of additional brain damage. The emergency veteran physician pondered whether or not to put his patient into a medically-induced coma.

But the "mind-reader" squeezed his hand, Estrella's way of saying -no need- I'll get through this with your help.

Under general anesthesia, the high-risk patient underwent emergency surgery to remove the bullet lodged in her skull. By a hair's breadth, the round had missed entering brain tissue. The patient was sutured with dissolvable stitches, for the second-degree tearing of the inside of her vagina and rectum. Following surgery, the critical patient received high doses of penicillin for the prevention of infection and the possibility of sexually-transmitted diseases. The extensive bruising to her breasts and lacerations across her nose and mouth, from physical assaults, would heal in time the medical expert summarized. But what could be done for inevitable mental trauma would not be addressed at this time, and neither would the mounting medical bill.

How the patient was going to pay for this medical treatment would have been furthest from an inconsolable mind.

Estrella would not know that Father Gonzales had offered to pay for her treatment.

The empathic man was at her bedside in the recovery room when she opened her eyes. She hazily reflected on another priest, about whom her mother had spoken so lovingly—Father Juan. Estrella looked into the face of the man who had saved her and *trusted* him. She confided, "Those pure evil soldiers stole everything from me...", she exhaled slowly, "my virginity, my foster brothers, and my identity as a human being. I was nothing more than a piece of meat to them."

Gonzales lowered his head, saddened to hear this amount of sorrow but, at the same time, riddled with guilt. He now, for some unknown reason, felt that he had wrongly misjudged her of being a sorcerer.

How could he possibly have answers to the spiritual plane from which "gifted with insight" souls are born?

The holy man took hold of her little hand. "I'm so sorry for what has happened to you," he said softly. "We must pray to God to ease your suffering: Our father, who art in Heaven..."

Estrella withdrew her hand, thus ending the priest's well-meaning supplication. "No, I will not pray to a God who *allowed* this evil to happen!" At the back of her mind, she also questioned why her grandmother, Kayapa, or the sacred spirit tree entity, had not come to her aid.

But the sacred whisperings of the tree spirits had visited her!

Estrella's depleted spiritual energy had prevented unearthly support.

Father Gonzales sighed with resolve. "I will pray for you so that your heart and soul will heal."

"Do you what you must, but my heart tells me that your prayers will be in vain. I have closed the door on religion."

The priest slipped out of the ICU.

༺༒༻

The persistent insistence by hospital officials for the local policía to investigate Estrella's sexual assault was brushed aside because of understaffing. The elderly emergency doctor shook his head as he thought about men, women, and children raped during the ongoing war: traumatic experiences that had now reached epidemic proportions in El Salvador. A humanitarian, the Columbian-born physician was baffled as to why the government was doing nothing about these heinous atrocities.

Because they are the culprits of the escalating crimes, his inner voice reasoned.

༺༒༻

Back then, CODIS—Combined DNA Index System—the science of solving crimes by using DNA, (deoxyribonucleic acid), from human paternal, and maternal chromosomes, was not available in Central America at this time. However, the quick-thinking ER doctor was determined to preserve the physical evidence, for the time when this remarkable science, did become available in Central America. So, he ordered blood, semen, and saliva samples to be collected. Her clothing, mainly her underwear, was also taken into evidence and, secured in plastic bags.

Estrella's rape-kit would remain in the hospital's cold storage facility for many years, until the day, when the CODIS database revealed a match.

⁕

During Estrella's lengthy surgery, the elderly neurosurgeon stated to a colleague, "I trust that I live long enough to see punishment for this brutal rape—" He sighed before adding, "But then I suppose that is wishful thinking."

In the critical care unit, Estrella continued to make a remarkable recovery. Her only complaint was that she was unable to have a bowel movement without crying out in pain.

Before being released, her mental health un-addressed, Estrella, became "numbed" to what had previously occurred at the residence. In a deep depression, she felt that she had nothing left of her past to hang onto. Forgetting who she was, what she was, the loss of all family members, and what had happened, became essential. This internal direction would assist in her survival.

Estrella wanted to get as far away from Masahaut as possible and spoke of her plans to her only visitor, Father Gonzales. The concerned priest queried, "Where will you go? It is the only home you've ever known, and the crops need to be grown for you to live."

Estrella's eyes smiled mischievously. "Oh, I have other ways to survive, and you know what I mean!"

Gonzales shook his head but chose not to comment out load. But contrary to his Catholic beliefs, a thought did enter into his mind: *If her fortunetelling practice kept her alive, then so be it.*

◦ļ◦

Five days later, the hospital released its patient. Estrella gratefully thanked the hospital staff for saving her life. She also thanked Father Gonzales for taking care of the medical bill and the clothing that he had provided for her. "I will repay you as soon as I am able," she promised.

"Don't let this worry you, my child. Please turn to God."

"No way, Jose!" read her facial expression.

◦ļ◦

On this sultry day, wearing brown and white checkered men's pants and a shirt altered to fit by Father's Gonzales seamstress, Estrella stepped onto a bus for the first time since the fateful bus ride to San Salvador City when she was little. The charitable donations of cash collected on her behalf by the hospital staff had aided her mission.

Forty minutes later, Estrella, with a straw hat covering the still bald surgical patch, alighted from the bus.

The woman with a new outlook on life began the long trek on foot, up Izalco, the youngest volcano in El Salvador.

During the nineteenth century, oceangoing sailors had set their course by the continuing glow from Izalco's summit, nicknaming it: "Lighthouse of the Pacific." The nurse had informed Estrella that this is where she might locate the left-wing, Cuban-backed rebel fighters, but couldn't guarantee this. The revolutionists frequently moved to avoid detection.

Estrella wondered if the insurgents would accept her. Would they mock her diminutive stature? Or would they welcome another rebel filled with revengeful hatred? How did her quest to be a part of the fighters come about?

While in recovery, a nurse loaned Estrella a battery-operated radio. She had turned the dial to one of the radio stations: "Radio Venceremos," an underground broadcast inciting public support. After listening to the "heated" shows, Estrella made up her mind. What better way than to seek retribution for the crimes committed against her. But she had no knowledge what role the FMLN "Sandinistas" women played in male-dominated El Salvador.

◯◠◡

Quite out of breath on the steep upward climb, Óscar Romero's last words echoed in Estrella's mind: *"I do not believe in death without resurrection. If they kill me, I will be resurrected in the Salvadoran people."*

His profound statement is what reinforced Estrella's determination to push upwards and join the fighters.

How could Estrella ever forget the day that Óscar died? She and her mother had narrowly escaped death, but sadly most of the Lozano family had not. What brought her to tears on this day was the flashback of another heinous act—the rape and cold-blooded murder of four churchwomen—following Archbishop Óscar Romero's assassination.

*

December 2, 1980, seven months after the murder of Archbishop Romero, four American nuns—, Ita Ford, aged 40, and Maura Clarke, aged 49. (Sisters from New York); Dorothy Kazel aged 40 (an Ursuline nun from Cleveland); and missionary volunteer, Jean Donavan aged 27 (a Catholic lay worker from Connecticut) had no perception that their lives on earth would be cut short.

How could they know that they were "marked" for death?

In the disturbing mindset of the Salvadoran military, churchwomen were synonymous with being subversive political activists, aiding the Communist insurgents. These churchwomen, victims of Salvadoran military insanity, became targets for assassination.

Late that evening, Jean Donavan, with Dorothy Kazel accompanying her, drove the white minibus to San Salvador International Airport. She was to pick up Sisters Ita and Maura, who was returning from a church conference in Nicaragua. A few miles outside the airport, the van came to a halt at a checkpoint. Unexpectedly, a tactical military truck sideswiped the minibus, forcing it off the road. The terrified women prayed: "Lord, we are here with open hands and open hearts, ready to depend on you for protection."

Acting on the orders of General Carlos Vides Casanova of the National Guard, five low-ranking soldiers forced the churchwomen in a spate of fearful tears, from the mini-van at gunpoint.

The four women had been savagely beaten, raped, and executed at close range.

Peasant farmers living nearby heard machine-gun fire followed by single shots and didn't know what to make of it so late at night. One farmer observed a white van, with lights on, and the radio blaring drive past his homestead.

The following morning, two farm workers discovered their bodies alongside an isolated road. Later, on the orders of a uniformed military officer, the remains were buried in a common grave. And that same day, their white van was discovered twenty miles away, burned and gutted.

One farmworker broke his silence.

Forty-eight hours later, their bodies were exhumed from the shallow grave in front of reporters, along with a crowd of horrified onlookers.

"It was the military who done it," accused a bystander.

"It was the National Guard," another man claimed.

"My son was stopped at the same checkpoint," a woman piped up. "He told me that he saw the uniformed soldiers ram a white van."

"Then they have a special place reserved for them in Hell," a reporter uttered. "Only sick-minded bastards rape and shoot nuns."

❧

In 1980 alone, nearly 10,000 Salvadoran citizens, mostly peasants, were assassinated by the National Guard.

By the end of the war in 1992, 75,000 lost their lives.

❧

Half-way up the steep volcanic slope, Estrella's tears fell in torrents, as the faces of her loved ones—her father, mother, brothers, and sisters, foster brothers, and her beloved little dog flashed into memory. The thought that they were all gone stirred up many emotions— loneliness, bitterness, anger, but most of all, hatred of the vile acts committed.

With adrenalin surging, Estrella ran as fast as her shortened legs would allow.

Was she making the right choice?

Would her spur of the moment decision to join the communist rebels, come back to haunt the little person in time to come?

That would be in the hands of *amor fati*—love of one's fate.

Would this mystical spinning of predetermined events clash with the little person for the rest of her life?

Chapter Twenty-Three

Izalco Rebel Encampment

- APRIL 30, 1990 -

"One is free to make whatever choice one wants, but one is not free from the consequences of the choice."
-Anonymous

Nearby, the eagle eyes of a trained "spotter" observed Estrella's every movement with suspicion. The encampment sentry was perplexed. She ran to her superior, announcing, "A child is coming our way."

The rebel fighter leader peered through her binoculars. Flabbergasted, she blurted, "It's not a child, it's a…"

She inhaled sharply. "It's a woman *dwarf!* What on earth is *she* doing here?"

"She's coming to join us," a youngster piped up.

"Or she's a spy!" another stated.

Dalia Mariá Guerra's voice went up two tones, "I will soon find out!"

The short, muscular woman hurriedly mounted a white horse and galloped off.

After the exhausting trek up the mountainside, the out of breath, Estrella approached the summit. She was unprepared for the "surprise" that awaited her. Startled, the weary traveler let out a booming shriek. "You nearly scared me to death," she scolded the horseback rider, who had her rifle aimed at Estrella's chest.

"Who are you, and why are you here?" Dalia demanded, her eyes sizing up the small woman.

Estrella looked her over twice.

Her "spooker," with masculine features—big leg and arm muscles, sharp jawline, and sporting fine mustache hairs, was indeed intimidating. Undoubtedly, she was someone not to cross!

Restraining her fright, Estrella blurted out, "I'm here because I want to join up, fight to kill the National Guard." She made eye contact. "I want to blow the heads off the two bastards that raped me, took my brothers, and burned my home!"

Was she believable?

She didn't expect the response of this the wide-eyed woman.

Dalia lowered her weapon and jumped off the horse. Then, she raised the less–than–four–foot Estrella into her arms and cradled her as if she were a baby. "My heart bleeds for you," she said sincerely. "We FMLN women (whose motto was: *The hour of the poor ... the hour of women*) welcome you to join us. We are pleased to have you fight with us. If you ever spot the bastards who did this, I will personally help you blow them to pieces."

Dalia lifted Estrella onto the saddle, mounted behind her, and galloped back to the encampment that was only reachable by a treacherous gnarly dirt pathway. With Dalia's strong arms holding onto her, Estrella, although untrusting, hadn't felt so protected in a long while.

When the riders arrived at the forested hideout, Estrella's eyes gazed upon the place that was now her home. A prickle of briars camouflaged the entrance to several caves used as, temporary dwellings. Unbeknownst to Estrella, the fighters never stayed in one place longer than a few days. The hideout, with spectacular views of lakes and streams, was tucked away on a steep hillside surrounded by tall fir trees that lashed and crashed against each other in a windstorm. Food supplies were hung in the branches to avoid scavenging by hungry critters. The scrabbling of geckos' on the tree limbs met Estrella's ears as the riders dismounted.

After Estrella's introduction to the twenty women fighters under her command, Dalia introduced the little person and her reasons for joining them.

"We all feel for you," a grandmotherly woman said. "Many here are rape survivors. You are safe now. Come, I will give you something to eat and drink…"

"How did it happen?" a young girl interrupted.

The last thing Estrella wished was to return to the darkest day in her life, so she simply fell asleep.

Since arriving at the encampment, Estrella loved the female companionship. She was content with being cherished as a human being, not a misshapen dwarf, by her *new* family. But there were moments when her thoughts strayed to her mother and father, siblings, and foster brothers. She missed the boys dreadfully and, wondered if they were still surviving the harsh wartime.

Before Estrella's "approval" into the FMLN side of high-risk activism, she underwent *"foreo,"* an assigned duty: stealing from shops, dropping off boxes without knowing their contents. Fifty-year-old, Dalia, advised the recruit that she'd be watching.

And the leader wasn't disappointed. Estrella was a pro as if she had been undertaking criminal activities all her life. Finally, the little person was entirely accepted.

When not participating in "stealing" missions, Estrella stayed behind, attending to the wounded and helping with the cooking. She lived day to day, in hideouts that changed regularly. Dalia made sure that they never spent more than two days in the same spot.

But as time passed, Estrella became restless. She confronted Dalia, "I wanted to become an armed guerilla, not a *molendera* (cook)."

"I don't think you are yet ready," Dalia commented.

"Yes, I am," pouted Estrella, even though she had never fired a weapon. "I have the blood of my warrior grandmother, Kayapa, who was born in the Amazon rainforest."

Estrella's life had been wrapped in a riddle until her mother had disclosed the contents of Belicia's journal. She was now willing to share her incredible and amazing ancestry with Dalia. The leader didn't move a muscle. She listened intently to Estrella as she repeated Analena's words, "Your grandmother, my mother, Kayapa, was an exceptional person. She possessed supernatural gifts passed to her from beyond this world. I do believe that you've been handed down this "awakening" from her, so use it wisely."

Dalia was fascinated. "I wish I had met your grandmother," she said. "She would have been a great asset to our cause. But, are you a *bruja* (witch), or a mind reader?"

Estrella laughed. "I'm not a witch. I have telepathic abilities. I sense what people are feeling and thinking. I can also foretell destinies. And I was once called *El Sabadora* "The Healer.""

Dalia frowned. "Really!" she remarked. "Then, how come you didn't see your own "path," the one that has broken you so?"

"I don't know the answer to that," Estrella replied truthfully. "Maybe I'm not "allowed" to see my destiny, only those of others!"

Dalia immediately thrust her palm out. "Okay, read mine."

Estrella began: "The Life Line indicates you are highly resistant to disease. So your health is not at risk." Dalia smiled.

"The Head Line indicates that you have a strong mental and psychological development. In other words, you are headstrong." Dalia grinned.

"The Heart Line indicates that you have a self-centered approach to love. You are consumed by the need to be loved."

"Not by men," Dalia scoffed. "I prefer to be loved by *women*."

The palm reader didn't comment. For she already knew Dalia had never been in any relationship with a man but was having a "forbidden" love affair with another rebel woman, younger than herself.

Estrella was about to read the next, which was the Sun Line, but her palm-reading gift took her to a dark place. She *saw* the U.S. helicopter being shot down by a rebel soldier, using a shoulder-held missile launcher in nine months to come. The pilot died in the crash, and the other wounded airmen were shot dead at the scene. She *saw* FMLN female fighters, dressed in combat fatigue, collecting a cache of weapons from the downed helicopter. Dalia was one of the raiders. Estrella *saw* her being arrested later by the National Guard and executed.

Puzzled by the sudden quietness, Dalia said, "I can see it in your face that you are hiding something from me. What is it? What have you seen in my palm? I don't care what it is, just tell me!"

"I have seen your ending," Estrella sadly replied. Regardless of the woman's tough exterior, Estrella admired and loved her. "Dalia, I beg you not to become involved in shooting down a U.S. helicopter in time to come…"

Dalia abruptly pulled her hand away. "I never did believe in this *mierda* (shit), so I have wasted precious time listening to it."

Estrella just heaved a sigh. She *knew* that women like Dalia paved the way for the re-conceptualization of the roles and the status of all women in El Salvador. Still, the mind reader *knew* that most of these Soviet and Cuban-backed communist rebels she was presently sharing life with, would not survive the wrath of the military National Guard defenders.

What Estrella wasn't allowed to see was her own demise!

Having been excluded from dangerous missions, Estrella spent most mornings shaking out spiders hiding in their clothing and footwear and at night, doing what she did best—fortune-telling. She had a captive audience, mainly among girls ranging in age from twelve to twenty, some of whom had attended universities. Their bright minds were willing to learn from Estrella about the capabilities of a "gifted" brain. Estrella vouched all humans had insight at birth, but some didn't know how to tune into them. But she did not wish to reveal her other gift—spiritual healing of those who had severe medical afflictions. She was worried that if her "healing" didn't cure a soldier, then she may be at risk of ridicule or worse.

෴

Three weeks later, the worse happened.

Estrella was nauseous. Like clockwork, upon awakening, she fled outside to throw up. This conduct didn't go unnoticed. Dalia approached Estrella after one of her vomiting bouts. "The oldest of our women, Lourdes, knows how to rid you of the unwelcome baby growing inside you," Dalia said, gesturing towards a grand-motherly figure who was, warming her hands over an open fire.

Estrella was speechless. Up to now, she had given no thought to the possibility of being pregnant by one of the soldiers. Now, it was a reality. She burst into tears. Dalia wrapped her soothing arms around Estrella, "Hush, little woman, I can relate to your pain." The guerrilla leader continued to tell the devastated Estrella something deeply personal. "When I was fourteen years old, my uncle raped me, and my mother didn't believe me. She said I was a slut and, got pregnant by a boy I was fond of at school. She told me that she was going to contact our priest to have me sent away to a home for unwed mothers. I ran away and sought out a backyard abortionist just like Lourdes, who is not of the Catholic faith. She is a Muslim."

The softly-spoken Lourdes gently touched Estrella's abdomen. "There is always a risk to your life in terminating unwanted pregnancies, but you are in good physical shape, so I don't see a problem. And I will treat you with strong antibiotics should an infection present itself."

Unease creased Estrella's features.

"It's your choice," Dalia added. "Whatever you decide, we women will stand by you."

"You should sleep on it," the abortionist concluded.

⁂

Six months later, Estrella birthed a healthy button-nosed baby girl, who showed no signs of achondroplasia. The proud new mother couldn't have cared less about *how* her child was conceived. And so, the memory of this conception was washed away by motherly adoration.

Estrella's features glowed. She was over the moon with this new addition to her family lineage. After birthing, the proud mother often lay awake, just looking at her baby.

She was named Aminta, after Archbishop Romero's late sister, who died in infancy. Estrella's daughter thrived in the love of her rebel family. Mother and child wanted for nothing. But their nomadic lifestyle began wearing Estrella down.

Since Aminta, of natural height, had been born in January 1991, they had uprooted five times. Estrella now longed for a more stable life for her daughter than living in hideouts that could never cater adequately to a child's growing needs.

Late one night, in an altered state of consciousness, Estrella had a vision. Once more, she *saw* the rebels blowing up El Salvador's third-largest bridge, Las Canas, which lay north of San Salvador. Just as she had predicted the day, she had *read* Dalia's palm. The psychic *saw* the blowing up of power lines, factories, the destruction of coffee plantations, and anything else that could damage the economy or support the El Salvadoran government. She *saw* the FMLN fighters' murder government officials. She knew that the rebel fighters, including her "innocent" self, were going to be held responsible for five percent of cruel civilian murders, including the killing of Jesuit priests, after the war. Estrella *saw* hundreds of decomposing bodies. But it was the tiny dead body of a five-month-old baby among the decomposing flesh that snapped the new mother out of the chilling precognition.

But the voice beyond the grave was not going to be silenced: *"Leave now before you and your child are added to the death toll to come."*

Estrella realized she had made a mistake becoming part of the guerilla effort. The mother had to act to save herself and her child.

The next day, well before sunrise, Estrella sneaked out of the hillside hideaway, without looking back to see if anyone had heard her. Holding baby Aminta to her bosom, she furtively weaved in out of the trees and dense bushes.

"La Mancha Mama and Kayapa, keep us safe," the little person implored.

With no money, no place to go, and no one she could contact for help, Estrella felt alone in her quest to leave the hillside. However, with intense uncertainty, she was more scared of homelessness than the apprehension she had felt when birthing Aminta. She wanted so badly to go home, but then had a change of heart. To return to Masahaut, a place that held the worst of nightmares, was perilous.

She had a flashback: While she had lain ill in the hospital, Father Gonzales informed her, that the soldiers had returned after learning that she was still alive.

Had the soldier's come back to finish her off once and for all? Returning home was definitely out, of the question.

A troubled mind continued to sap her energy. How was she going to take care of herself and Aminta, without a roof over their heads? Where they will be spending the next nights became a daunting prospect.

Suffering from pain from a plantar wart jutting out from the sole of her bare right foot, Estrella reached the small, municipal market town of Los Apoyos. There, on the streets and penniless, she joined other wretched souls begging for food and loose change, in unbearable humidity. The baking temperature was the least of her concerns. She hoped Dalia or another member of the "crew" didn't spot her—

Loud grumbling sounds from her empty stomach took precedence over that thought. Estrella was hungry. But her priority was to use any money she got to buy warmer clothes for her baby when night temperature could fall drastically. Baby Aminta had on a handmade cotton onesie, not suitable for nighttime weather.

Even in a country of short people, the dwarf race was not a common sight. Clutching her six-month-old baby, the little person became the target of stares. Children accompanying their mothers publically harassed Estrella, with ill-behaved comments:

"She's smaller than me, and I'm five," a girl said.

"She's so ugly," added her younger sibling.

"So is her baby," her brother remarked, with an "*ugh*" expression.

Estrella sighed. She wasn't fazed at all by these derogatory comments. They weren't anything new. So she smiled smugly responded, "At least I'm cute. I can't say the same for you. You are as ugly as a frog!"

The mother of the ill-behaved children glared at Estrella but still threw a few coins her way.

It was beginning to get dark. The market traders were packing up, and shoppers were going home. Estrella checked her donation proceeds. The loose change would buy two small veggie tacos and a bottle of water. She kicked herself for not applying her palm-reading talent because it would have at least afforded a backpackers' hostel room.

Now, her first homeless night was filled with dread.

Seated against the trunk of a large tree, with baby Aminta tucked beneath her *serape* (Mexican blanket), Estrella was fraught with fear when she heard the foul-mouthed chitchat of a street gang nearby. Would they hurt her and her baby? She just couldn't face another degrading experience.

No one should ever have felt that agonized, but Estrella did.

She was just about to flee to somewhere safer when a tall, gray-haired man approached. "Little mother, you can't stay here," the soft-spoken man said in a concerned tone. "It's much too dangerous. Follow me. I'm poor like you. I make a little money cleaning the market square after hours. My wife and I live with eight relatives in an old house, but I do have an old car you can stay in for the time being."

Beggars' can't be choosers.

A mentally and physically worn-out Estrella meekly walked alongside the stranger. She did, however, have good vibes about this kind man, whose gentle voice was comforting, "My name is Bastien Olivares, and my wife's name is Analena. But she likes to be called Anna."

Estrella's heart welled up with sadness. Inner words spoke her feelings: *I would give you everything I have just to feel your warm arms around me.* Estrella shook off her thoughts, addressing her benefactor. "I am Estrella Godwin Lozano My daughter's name is Aminta," she said, exposing the sleeping baby's chubby face.

"She is beautiful," Bastien said.

Estrella smiled. "Yes, she is. Thank goodness she doesn't look like me, or have my little body," the proud mother laughed play-fully. "We are grateful for your kindness."

"No need to thank me. We must look out for each other in these bad times."

Along the way, Bastien asked her some personal questions: What had brought her to homelessness? Was she married, and if so, where was her husband? Were her parents alive? Did she have relatives? Was she the only little person in the family?

Oddly, Estrella found herself opening up to this person, a man she hardly knew. The weight of bitterness off her chest was comforting.

Estrella, however, omitted the sexual assault, something she wished never again to revisit outspokenly. It had taken her heart and soul, back then.

"Oh, what sadness and so much loss you have gone through," Bastien said. He, too, found himself opening up. "I know the feeling of loss all too well. The military took my five stepsons, but not the youngest, Julio. He ran away from home at the age of eleven. So luckily he wasn't there when the National Guard turned up."

"He was fortunate," said Estrella. "You said you have stepchildren. Do you have children with Analena?"

"No. I married my sister-in-law when my younger brother deserted her and the children. I went to see him at the military base. I begged him to go home to his family. He refused. Analena reached out to me for help with the children. She had two jobs, doing laundry for the rich during the day, and at night, working in a factory making military uniforms seven days a week. I knew Anna's health was declining rapidly, and the children were badly neglected, so I moved in and became a husband and father. We have been together ever since. Living in sin, the parish priest informed us. We don't go to church anymore."

Estrella did not comment.

Bastien continued, "I have not seen or spoken to my brother since the day I confronted him at the base. I learned that he spends most of his time in the company of prostitutes…"

His sentence ended. An index finger gestured to a dilapidated house with a corrugated iron roof.

"I must warn you it is crowded. You see, family who found themselves badly off since the war came to live with us. Another thing is that my poor wife is not well in the head. So if she doesn't greet you, think nothing of it. Okay?"

"Oh, maybe I can fix that," Estrella claimed.

Bastien's bushy eyebrows knotted. "I don't understand."

"I'm blessed with healing powers," she replied. "I will try to make her well again."

Bastien's face lit up with joy.

The tiny home was cramped with bodies ranging from their fifties to eighties.

Bastien introduced Estrella. The family didn't stare at the stranger; instead, they greeted the little person with such warmth in their voices. Estrella was elated.

She was introduced to Anna, who had decided to stay in her bed, refusing to get up. It was evident that the poor woman's mind was not on this planet. "Gracias, you have found my baby," Anna said gleefully. Then, she stretched her arms, out, "Pass him to me."

Noticing Estrella's astonished expression, Bastien quickly explained, "She thinks your baby is her missing child, Julio. We are not sure if the National Guard captured him…" Bastien sighed heavily. "I believe he may no longer be with us."

Estrella's thoughts strayed to her foster brothers: *Were they alive? Were the boys leading a hellish life as child soldiers?* She could relate to this wretched woman and addressed Bastien. "Then, I must help her overcome the loss, with my special healing gifts."

Bastien and Anna's church-going Catholic relatives, who had gathered in the bedroom, looked at him for an explanation. "Estrella is a psychic healer, El Sabadora, sent by the angels. With their help, she is going to try and cure poor Anna of her psychological darkness."

There were mixed expressions on faces. No one said a word. The warm hospitality she had received would soon turn sour.

With doubtful expressions focused on her, Estrella seated herself next to Anna on the bed and began to access healing powers by, running her fingers across Anna's forehead. Still mesmerized by the baby in her lap, the out-to-lunch woman didn't feel the El Sabadora's touch as her fingers made a connection between their two energies, reaching the woman's tired, aching wounded spirit. The healer was able to identify Anna's malaise. It seemed she was harboring a deep resentment of abandonment by her first husband and the guilt of neglect for her children, whom she had given no time, especially young Julio, whom she adored. He, like his father, had left home and never returned.

In the quiet of the bedroom, gasps of disbelief came from Estrella's audience. In front of them, Anna bathed in a glowing violet aura. Within seconds, the astral energy of pure light successfully dissolved the adverse energy pathways that had flowed within the bitter Anna. She returned to the real world, with her spirit and body back in balance.

Now restored, with love, warmth, and humor, Anna was a different person. Bastien, who had loved her before she married his brother, couldn't have been happier. "Thank you from the bottom of my heart, Estrella. You will not sleep in my old car. I will give up my bed for you and your baby."

Although the onlookers had been mesmerized, Anna's mother was having none of it. "Is this the work of Satan?" she asked Estrella. Before the healer could utter a response, Anna's female relatives voiced their own opinions:

"I believe God sent El Sabadora to us," one claimed.

"Whoever sent her, I'm elated to see that dear Anna is back to her cheerful self," said another.

"I disagree," said Anna's grandmother. "I believe that she is a sorcerer."

"We must all pray to deliver us from her witchcraft!"

Bastien stepped in, "I don't care what you think of our guest. She has brought my beautiful wife back to me, and I'm grateful to her."

⚮

In the time following Anna's miraculous return, Estrella was living off the kindness of this family, until her "unique" powers became known to others outside this home. Her talent had reached the ears of other sick persons, who now flocked to the Olivares' modest home.

A revitalized Anna took care of Aminta as Estrella went about curing psychological and physical maladies. Payment for her "services" poured into the household, which provided a larger house in the same area. And not one of the relatives denounced her powers now!

Life improved for all of the players.

Months passed, and just before Christmas, for all her new-found contentment, nothing could have prepared Estrella for what she discovered in Bastien's and Anna's bedroom.

She spotted a black and white photograph propped up on a shelf. What she saw didn't sit well with the shocked Estrella. She stared in horror and disbelief. *It can't be! Yes*, her brain screamed, *your eyes are not deceiving you!* Feeling sick to her stomach, she clamped a hand across her mouth to prevent a scream from alerting the whole household.

Stamped on her brain was the face of one of her rapists, looking back at her from the wedding photo. In victim-mode, Estrella's chest tightened with a rage so deep that it physically hurt, causing her breathing to become erratic. What she should do about this upsetting discovery was not at all clear.

Clutching the old photo in hand, she fled from the room.

A winded Estrella stepped outside the home to catch her breath and collect her thoughts. She *had* to know what they knew. Was *he* still in contact with them? Did Anna know where to find him?

Estrella could no longer hold her disturbed feelings.

She found Anna preparing the evening meal and said, directly, in a calm voice, "Anna, I need to get something off my chest, and you are not going to like what I have to say."

Anna's eyes squinted. "What is it?" she asked.

"Why do you keep this wedding photo," Estrella queried, placing the picture on the table. "Since you made a new life with his brother, I find this strange."

Estrella wasn't expecting the defensive reaction. "Why wouldn't I keep a photo of happy times? After all, *he* is the father of my children, not Bastien."

Estrella intended to handle her thoughts delicately, but incensed emotions overruled her. She ripped the photo into pieces, letting out her pent-up anger, "Your husband, the man in the photo, violated me! Raped me! And Aminta could be his daughter!"

Estrella's volatile outburst took a few moments to sink in. Then, looking very uncomfortable, Anna heatedly disagreed, "My Julio would never rape anyone. I should know. I was married to him for twenty years." She balled a fist. "You imagined it!"

Affronted by Anna's last remark and hand gesture, a furious Estrella snapped, "You might think you know everything about him, but you don't, because he *is* my rapist! So tell me, doesn't the company he now keeps, prostitutes, tell you something?"

Analena's silence echoed a statement of denial!

Estrella wondered why she had expected the woman to accept that her husband had been an evildoer! What happened at the adobe house had never left her.

Now the little person went from being a family member to a foe.

Her blood boiling, Anna shrilled at the top of her voice, "Get out of my home! You ungrateful *puta* (bitch)! We took you in as one of our family, and now you accuse my husband of being a rapist. Leave and do not return!"

Estrella glared at Anna. Hadn't she "saved" this woman's life?

She reluctantly decided Anna was never going to accept that Julio was a rapist!

Anna continued to rant and rave loudly, bringing family members into the kitchen.

"What's all the noise?" asked Anna's father.

"This stinking *midget* is accusing Julio of raping her," spat Anna. "She is a liar! You all know him. He would never harm a woman, let alone a shriveled-up ugly dwarf!"

Estrella had nothing more to say.

Their face-to-face confrontation had been for nothing. The only way this little woman could put the shattered pieces of her life back together was to remain silent.

There would be no victory this day.

Estrella gently lifted the sleeping Aminta from the cozy cradle that Bastien had made for her, packed a few belongings, and retrieved a wad of *colones* stashed under a bed. In a way, she was glad that Bastien was not at home when the altercation had occurred. As far as she knew, he was in the city buying groceries.

Sobbing endlessly with reopened traumatic wounds, Estrella and eleven-and-a-half month-old Aminta boarded a bus heading for the capital of, San Salvador. Estrella was painfully aware that without *cédulas* (travel IDs) enforced by the El Salvadoran government, she could be pulled from the bus and arrested. It was forbidden to travel between towns and cities without a permit. Her directive was to head for the *avuntamiento* (town hall) and plead for official documents to depart El Salvador. She wanted to leave her country of birth if it was the last thing she ever did in her life. But would the bureaucrats even care if her birth and baptism certificates had gone up in flames at the adobe? And the official was bound to query why she had traveled to the capital when a cédula could only be issued in place of her birth. However, there was a more pressing problem—how she was going to explain why no birth certificate was in existence for Aminta either.

A strong-minded Estrella had to give it her best effort.

Where there is a will, there is a way!

Chapter Twenty-Four

San Salvador City

- TWO DAYS BEFORE NAVIDAD, 1991 -

"Only the mind cannot be sent into exile."
—UNKNOWN

With Aminta straddled on her hip, Estrella walked across the main square, and into an old stone building. It once housed an infamous prison and now stockpiled an arsenal of weapons for the National Guard. She waited two hours before being ushered towards a desk. She looked in dismay. The chair with, the height of a barstool, was way too high for her shortened limbs. Cheeks flushing with frustration, there was no way she was going to ask for help from this unsmiling official.

Standing while, holding a heavy child, she poured out her circumstances to the exhausted-looking man, who had swollen bags under his eyes. *You need a good night's sleep more than me,* Estrella silently mused, then continued, "I have no mother, father, or living relatives to go to, and as I have told you everything I owned went up in flames."

The desperate mother's plight became briskly refuted.

"Without your two birth certificates, no passport for you or your baby can be issued," the unsmiling official stated. Then, he looked belligerently at her. "I *warn* you that if you *try* to travel without an official ID, you will be arrested, or worse, shot!"

A crestfallen mother exited the public building. Her heart pumped fretfully. She was uncertain of what to do next. Returning to the rebels or going home to Masahaut Pueblo was out the question.

Estrella spotted an unoccupied bench in the courtyard and seated herself and Aminta, who was wailing with hunger. From her shoulder bag, she retrieved the last of the milk bottles she had prepared before leaving her former residence.

Aminta glugged contently as her mother gathered her *"what-to-do-next"* thoughts.

Was it a stroke of good fortune that *another* gray-haired man approached her?

"You seem, troubled little lady," the thin as a noodle man said. "Is there anything I can do to help?"

"I don't think anyone can help me," Estrella replied forlornly. "I'm so messed up!"

"What makes you think this way?" queried the stranger.

Estrella found herself leaving no stone unturned as she told of her past and present. He reminded her of the soft-spoken, good-hearted Bastien.

"I desperately wish to leave this hell hole of a country because I want to give my child a better life. But we have no birth certificates for *cédulas* to travel by bus or valid passports to leave El Salvador. As I've explained, my family home has been burned down by the National Guard, and my daughter is the product of rape. All I once had is gone."

The stranger was well aware that her child wasn't the first baby to be born of rape during these abysmal times. "Ah, all is not lost," he consoled. "Do you have any money?"

Estrella's eyes squinted with suspicion. She wasn't *well* educated but had been taught the basics of reading, writing, and arithmetic by her father. If her mind-reading talent had been operating, she would have discovered he was a former priest gone rogue. However, awareness did nudge Estrella. She cynically responded, "Don't my peasant clothing and lack of shoes give you a hint as to my financial situation?"

The unfrocked priest grinned. "Do not despair, brave little woman. I know of someone who can provide you with a good quality birth certificate for *cédulas* and passports, but he is not cheap. That's why I asked if you had money."

Lowering her precautionary guard, an excited Estrella asked, "How much will it cost?"

"One-hundred US dollars," Hernández replied.

"How much is that in *colones*?"

"I am not sure!" he honestly answered.

"I do have some *colones*," Estrella affirmed, "I just hope that they are enough!"

"You can exchange them for U.S. dollars at any bank," Hernández advised. "Then you will know if you have enough for the document fees. You don't have to hand over the money until the forger hands over the certificates."

Estrella heaved a sigh of relief. She thought that she might have more than the requested sum hidden in the lining of her one-piece luggage, a battered vintage 1950s hard-sided suitcase that she had "liberated" from Bastien's house.

"Wait here," Hernández instructed. "I'll be back shortly with *some* information."

Estrella remained seated on the concrete bench, to await his return. She certainly wasn't clued in to the fact that Hernández was the forger, also known as the "Doctor."

Fifteen minutes later, Hernández was back at Estrella's side.

That was quick!

"Here are his instructions," the rogue priest said. "I have to take photos."

Hernández retrieved a Polaroid camera from his pants pocket, and instructed Estrella, "Stand over there next to the wall. I will take your photo first and then of your child."

In the close-up photo, Aminta burst into tears as the bright flash pierced her eyes. "Sorry, child, it's all over now." Hernández soothed. To Estrella, he added, "Go now and exchange your money, and I'll take care of your daughter until you come back."

At first, Estrella hesitated. Should she leave her child with a stranger? But it seemed that Aminta was content in Hernández's company, happily sucking on a chocolate bar.

Fortunately, Estrella had more than enough money for the requested fee.

The American dollars and the residual *colones* notes tucked into her bra, Estrella rushed to the bench. There, Hernández delivered Estrella with further instructions. "Tomorrow morning, you must board the five o'clock bus going to Ahuachapán. It's a very long journey, so take plenty of water and food. I'll meet you at the Ahuachapán bus terminal around about 8:00 p.m., with the documents. Do you have somewhere to sleep for the night?"

"No, but I'll find someplace," Estrella answered.

"Good. I will see you tomorrow evening then."

❧

Mother and child roughed it under a bridge not far from the local bus depot.

The US exchange rate had taken a big chunk of her savings. What remained of her money had to take them to Mexico, as was her intention.

Under the bridge, Estrella encountered some friendly homeless people, who greeted her with warmth and without gawking at her. But that didn't stop Estrella from being fearful. What if a homeless person found her repugnant and attacked her? The thought of what could happen hastily prompted her next move.

Estrella and Aminta spent the night under lamplight, on the familiar concrete bench. She slept with one eye open.

Well before sunrise, Estrella, her back aching from sitting rigidly with Aminta on her lap, went in search of a street food vendor. She bought six *pupusas*—thick flatbread—filled with refried beans and *queso duro* (similar to mozzarella cheese) and bottled water. With the food supplies tucked into her shoulder bag, she and Aminta headed for the bus depot. Fifteen minutes later, seated at the back of an old U.S. built school bus, Estrella's small size again became the center of attention. Generally, she wasn't looked upon as a person, just a freak of nature. So the disparaging comments of the bus passengers weren't anything new.

"Do you think she's from a circus sideshow?" one traveler insultingly remarked.

Another answered, "A circus or fair hasn't been here since the war started."

"Well, she belongs in a freak show, like the three-legged man, the Siamese con-joined twins, and the bearded lady!" another ignorantly added.

"If that *is* her child, she's likely to be ugly and small, just like her mother," an overweight woman stated.

On and on went the derogatory remarks.

Estrella wanted to give these cruel individuals an equally offensive rebuttal to shut them up. But she chose instead to ignore them. Her hands and mind were full of her nearly one-year-old daughter's unruly behavior.

Having a temper tantrum, the toddler spat out the *pupusa* onto her mother's bare feet, shrilling, "No want this!"

How she was going to handle this hair-raising behavior on a long journey? Estrella didn't know.

"Aminta, stop it at once!" she scolded.

Several pairs of eyes turned towards the back of the bus. One woman's stare chilled Estrella. The frustrated parent flushed crimson with embarrassment.

The unruly child had undoubtedly caused further unwanted attention.

A *melano* (very dark-skinned, almost black) woman, halfway down the bus, got up out of her seat and came to the frustrated mother's side. "Would you like me to take her back to my seat for a while? I have six grandchildren and two great-grandchildren her age, and have long ago learned how to calm down fusses in children."

"Yes, please," Estrella said with a sigh of relief. "My child has had a lot of upheavals lately. Nothing I say or do quietens her."

The Ecuadoran-born great-grandmother smiled. "Oh, she is at that defiant testing age..." She paused as if trying to recall something. Then with a broad smile, she quoted what her mother had said, "The older they become, the worse they get!"

Estrella didn't know how to respond to that particular comment.

Aminta quietened as soon as Carmella lifted her into her arms and went back to her bus seat. Had Estrella inadvertently passed her anxiety onto her child? It sure seemed like it.

Having had no sleep the previous night on the uncomfortable bench, Estrella closed her weary eyes. But her hippocampus wasn't going to let her have any well-deserved rest. Flashback after flashback came forth from her memory bank, recounting her childhood to adulthood traumas. In an attempt to shrug off these unwanted memories, Estrella forced open her tired eyes and gazed at the outside scenery through the mud-splattered window. In the foreground, she saw billows of white smoke and steam pouring out of a cone-shaped volcano and rising into the clear blue sky.

Her immediate thought was: *I hope that it doesn't erupt before we reach the border.*

Finally, slumber overtook her, fading out her thoughts. Estrella snored softly.

She awoke suddenly an hour later, trying to remember where she was. Strangled by panic, Estrella broke out in nervous sweat. She looked around. The bus was empty of her fellow travelers.

Where were they? And where was her child!

Her short legs flew along the aisle, with her skirt billowing like the sky-borne, Mary Poppins. Outside in the fresh air, Estrella spotted her child sitting on the Good Samaritan Carmella's lap, chewing something. Estrella rushed over to them. "Why didn't you wake me?"

"I let you sleep," Carmella replied. "Your daughter is fine."

Estrella planted a soft kiss on Aminta's cheek, whose puckered expression indicated that she really couldn't care less about her mother's affection. Content with scoffing down a loaded refried bean burrito, and sucking from a bottle of fruit-flavored carbonated drink, a beverage Estrella would never have allowed her to consume, Aminta ignored her mother.

"You can be quite a brat," Estrella said humorously.

She walked to the food cart, and bought herself something to eat, returned, and chatted with the "fairy godmother."

Carmella asked, "Do you live in Ahuachapán?"

"No, I'm going to stay with relatives in Guatemala," Estrella lied. The less the woman knew about her clandestine trip, the better.

Estrella was not aware that Carmella happened to be a descendant of an Afro-Caribbean brujeria priestess, who had practiced witchcraft. The older woman *knew* of Estrella's quandary and scribbled some writing on a paper napkin. Passing it to Estrella, Carmella whispered, "If you need somewhere to stay, here's my address in Guatemala."

Estrella took the folded paper and tucked it into her bra. "Thank you. That's so very kind of you..."

The call from the driver to board the bus ended the conversation.

One hour later, the bus arrived at the city of Ahuachapán, bordering San Lorenzo and the Republic of Guatemala. Estrella said goodbye to Carmella, who had been a fantastic godsend. Not known at this time was that Carmella had been a former guard at the Pichincha prison that had once held Belicia Godwin. Had the elderly Carmella *known* this missionary? Did she know about the Amazonian baby who was Estrella's mother? The two women travelers would meet again, under different circumstances. The answers to these questions would be shocking.

⊄⊅

At the arranged meeting place, a roadside café, Estrella awaited her paperwork. She wasn't surprised to encounter the *same* man she had met outside the town hall. With her "gifted senses" back in action, Estrella now *knew* that Hernández was the actual forger. Without letting on, Estrella greeted him, "I'm glad to see you. Did you get them?"

Hernández smiled as he handed her the skillfully forged birth certificates and *cédulas*, along with un-watermarked passports. The former priest forewarned, "Show no nervousness because they are well trained in identifying illegals. Look the customs officer in the eye when handing over the passports, okay? And remember to follow my instructions when you leave the building. If you require emergency help, I have written the name and addresses of trusted contacts in Guatemala and Mexico, if you intend to travel further. I hope that you find peace in a new beginning. God bless you both."

Estrella looked around to make sure no one was watching. Then she put her hand under her flowery blouse and removed the wad of US bills from her bra. Handing the money over, she said, "I can't thank you enough for all you have done for my daughter and me. God bless you, too."

⊖

During the civil war, there were no cutting-edge computer networks that could confirm legitimacy or otherwise at Central American border crossings.

On this Christmas Eve in 1991, her knees trembled under her skirt as she, firmly grasping Aminta's hand, and waited in line at the *aduana* (customs).

Then, all hell broke loose.

Estrella's knees knocked, as she watched two heavy-built customs officers forcibly restraining and pinning a heavily tattooed young man to the ground.

Why the young man was under arrest, she could only guess.

As the police marched the young guy past her, a wide-eyed

Estrella thought that she had seen a ghost. The hairs on the back of her neck rose as if shocked by electricity. The young man was the spitting image of her rapist, Julio Olivares, except a much younger version. Estrella took two steps backward, bumping into the person behind her. "Oh, I'm sorry," she apologized to the annoyed senior.

She now focused her full attention on the captive. "I know who you are!" she yelled out. "You are Julio junior Olivares, right?"

Like an owl, the young man rotated his head. "Maybe," he returned arrogantly. "Why do you want to know?"

"I know your father!" she snarled. "He's a sick-minded bastard! If he is still alive, I hope he rots in hell!" The fixed stare in the fourteen-year-old could have sunk a ship.

Yanked forcibly forward, Loco made no further comment.

She had stared into *identical* eyes, back in Masahaut Pueblo. This teen's high cheekbones, genetic eye color, and his gait, a bilateral weakness with, dropping of the pelvis are all, characteristics memorized during her violation—enough proof for Estrella. He *was* indeed Julio junior, aka, Loco.

She quickly dispersed all past thoughts, to prepare herself for a different experience.

With her insides churning and hands visibly shaking, Estrella stood on tiptoes to slide over the fake passports through the booth window opening. The cigarette-smoking officer stared down at her. He had not had a dwarf come through the border before. "What is your purpose for crossing?" he asked, examining the passports.

"Visiting relatives" was Estrella's quick response.

The custom's official stamped the passports. "Go through," he said, gesturing to a side gate. Estrella thought that her racing heart would stop beating any minute. She had done it, got through the border without incident. A happy, Estrella stepped in line, hip-holding Aminta as she followed the other border crossers toward a bridge over the Suchiate River bordering Guatemala and Mexico.

As planned, she paid two US dollars to a resident to raft her over the river. It was better transportation than wading through a shallow stretch of water into Mexico, carrying a toddler as many of the lineup folk with children were doing.

Some days later, as luck would have it, she made it to Nuevo Laredo and to the address Hernández had handed her. Back at the roadside café, he said he had already been in contact with the owner, informing him that Estrella needed a place to stay until she could get back on her feet financially.

Estrella's good fortune would last until 2019. Would her daughter's fate be equal?

Chapter Twenty-Five

The Civil War Ends

- JANUARY 16, 1992 -

"There are many things that can only be seen through eyes that have cried."
—Archbishop Óscar Romero, 1917-1980

Twelve years of terrorization ended when the Chapultec Peace Accords were signed in Mexico City in 1992. For Estrella and thousands of other fleeing victims of this horrific, brutal war, the "drawing of the line in the sand"—was a little too late.

She had "moved on" for now.

Having trekked long distances across Guatemala and Mexico, Estrella and her child finally made it to a rural hilltop address in Nuevo Laredo, in the Mexican state of Tamaulipas. Her suitcase stolen at the last bus depot without, a cent, or a change of clothing to their names, Estrella gawked at the farmhouse hacienda, a luxurious sight she had never seen before. It was beyond any poor person's imagination.

Estrella stepped onto the wraparound porch and pressed the bell on the double doors.

The cattle rancher, DeLeon Padilla, a slim man whom Estrella reckoned to be in his early forties, greeted her, "Welcome to Nuevo Laredo. When my half-brother, Hernández, contacted me about you and your child fleeing from El Salvador, I spent sleepless nights worrying. But here you are…"

Aminta's little stomach let out a hungry howl. It broke DeLeon's sentence.

"Come in," he said. "I'll instruct my cook to prepare food for you both."

Aching legs, hungry bellies, and parched lips, Estrella and Aminta entered the Padilla hacienda. This beautifully-restored farmhouse was beyond imagination for someone who had lived with compacted dirt of softly-colored walls. Modern, stylish furniture bordered a double-sided fireplace, and a multitude of cowhides, scattered throughout the main living area, accentuated the rich tiled flooring. *Why did they need a woodstove in Mexico's stifling hot climate?*

She would soon have the answer.

Mouth agape in amazement, Estrella didn't at first notice the tall, slender woman enter. Dressed in luxury garments, thirty-year-old, Caitlin, a red-haired *gringa*, and daughter to an Irish mob boss approached Estrella and her husband. "Oh my goodness, you're no bigger than my five-year-old niece."

Unaccustomed to the English language and blue-eyed *gringas,* Estrella looked to DeLeon for translation. The owner of the Padilla Ranch introduced his spouse in Spanish, "This is my wife, Caitlin. She speaks very little Spanish. Maybe you will be able to teach her?"

"I am pleased to meet you, Señora Padilla," Estrella greeted with sincerity. Her politeness was snubbed, as the domineering Caitlin lashed out at her husband in English, "What were you thinking? You and Hernández are out of your minds letting her come here! She's filthy, smells like a dead horse, and her child has soiled herself. Get them out of my home before I order her thrown out!"

There was no need for translation. Estrella had *interpreted* this soulless woman's words. Caitlin's "discomfort" at having low-class peasants in her luxurious home didn't sit well with her husband. DeLeon's eyes narrowed. "Don't tell me what I can or can't do in my own home, woman!" he snapped. "Go about your business and leave me to mine."

The sound of Caitlin's high heels clip-clopping on the tiled floor echoed down the hallway as she, fumed, "How dare he talk to me like that, and in front of a disgusting misfit!"

Estrella stared at the retreating woman's stiffened back and concluded that her ungracious host suffered from psychotic delusions from her drug addiction—cocaine. But the gentle-natured little person wasn't offended. Instead, Estrella wondered if she could "fix" Caitlin, and change her back to the sweet, loving girl she once was.

Slim and none!

⚜

Alone outside the residence, mother and child were seated at the patio table on the luxurious green garden turf. The hungry pair consumed the splendid three-course meal that had been prepared by DeLeon's private chef, Gabor, a five-foot four-inch descendant of the Mayan people.

The chef couldn't help but stare at his hungry guests. His inner sensitivity voiced: *Probrecitos! (Poor things!) They probably haven't eaten a good meal in some time.*

His curiosity did, however, cause speculation.

These visitors were *not* the typical type of people his employers entertained. And, the affluent couple was *not* charitable: they've never invited anyone off the streets. So the mystery as to why this mother and child were here boggled the chef's mind: *Who was she? Was she just an impoverished relative, who had come here for help?* Gabor brushed his thoughts aside as he observed Estrella pick up a linen napkin and gently wipe food off her child's mouth and hands. His mother did the same to him when he of that age. He moved towards them, inquiring, "Have you had enough to eat?"

Estrella gratefully answered, "I couldn't put another morsel down, however hard I tried. Gracias, Señor. The food is the finest I have ever tasted. God bless you."

Gabor's dark-brown eyes shone with appreciation. "You are so welcome." Curiosity got the better of him, "I hope you don't mind my asking, but where are you from?"

"El Salvador," Estrella replied.

"What brings you to Mexico?" He clicked his tongue in reproach: *What a stupid question!* He had been watching that country's chaos and the hundreds of souls who had perished trying to flee the country on television for years.

"Oh, it's a long story that I do not wish to share at this moment," Estrella replied guardedly.

Gabor had one more thing to ask, "Are you relatives of Señor Padilla?"

"Heavens, no!" was Estrella's return.

"Well, I trust that your stay at Padilla Ranch goes well, and if you need anything, I live in a guest house just behind the hacienda. Please feel free to call anytime, that's if I'm not *slaving* in the kitchen…"

DeLeon's sudden appearance halted his chef's words.

"Come and see where you will be staying. I'll give you a couple of days to settle in. Then we can discuss how you are going to support yourself and your child."

"I'm a hard worker. Can I work for you?"

"Okay, I'll think of something," DeLeon returned vaguely.

A sated but tired mother and child climbed into the rear of a truck.

DeLeon drove to the far end of the Padilla estate. "Here we are," he announced, turning off the engine.

Estrella's eyes opened wide.

She noted six small gloomy abodes, jostled together. They paled in compassion to the modest adobe dwelling Estrella once had called *home*. These homes were constructed from recycled materials, cinderblocks, and cardboard, with tin roof coverings, held down by large boulders. Estrella wondered if they would not withstand any manifestations of Mother Nature's wrath: earthquakes and excessive winds, or heavy rainstorms.

These "sheds" were anything but inviting. Nevertheless, to Estrella's mind, it was not all doom and gloom. She wasn't in a country that nearly killed her.

Several pairs of eyes peered out at her from the broken windows.

"I'll introduce you to my farmworkers," DeLeon said, beckoning with a hand for the spies to come outside.

Estrella was introduced to DeLeon's farm manager, other farmhands, and their wives and children. At first, they stared at her small stature, but with warm voices, they welcomed the new arrivals.

Estrella followed DeLeon to the last shack at the end of the row. He pushed open the door that lacked a latch. "This one is yours. Get some sleep, and we will talk tomorrow."

"*Buenas noches* (Goodnight)," Estrella wished.

"*Buenas noches* to both of you," DeLeon echoed.

Estrella was pleasantly surprised to find that the interior of their home was nothing like the slum-like exterior. Surprisingly the shack had electricity, plumbing, a bathroom with a flushing toilet and a small shower cubicle, a tiny kitchen equipped with basic needs, and two beds in a back room.

Estrella was unaware that a family of four, the farmworker, his wife, and their two children, had been ousted out of the home shortly after her arrival. The "evicted" family now shared cramped conditions next door.

That first night in the chill of the dipping of night temperatures, Estrella shivered with the cold seeping into her bones. The firepit at the Padilla hacienda now made sense. But there was no such luxury in this cabin.

༄

The next day, Estrella became acquainted with her neighbors, whom she learned worked long hours for poor pay, while DeLeon and Caitlin lived in the lap of luxury.

Aminta played with other children when Estrella was put to work, cleaning and oiling the horse saddles belonging to the *vaqueros* (cattle herders), who rounded up and loaded beef cattle onto trucks for—subsequent transport to the U.S. border. The newly hired worker would soon learn that animals were not the only commodity loaded on these trucks. She wasn't surprised. How else could a cattle rancher live in such opulence?

༄

Nuevo Laredo, a trafficking corridor for cartels controlling routes in and out of the city, had long since added DeLeon to their payroll. It was, however, his wife's criminal organization connections that distributed the "product."

༄

After months of surviving on minimal wages, with little income remaining after payment of her rent, Estrella couldn't provide the basic needs for her growing child. The impoverished mother wanted a piece of "easy-pie." Her hands were leathery and sore from the constant use of saddle soap, a petroleum-based product, and she just wanted a better life than this daily grind. After one long day of toil, Estrella walked to the hacienda in search of her boss. Nearing the residence, she noticed some unfamiliar high-end luxury vehicles parked in the driveway. At the entrance to this home, two thick-set men with assault weapons and walkie-talkies (two-way radios transceivers being that there was no cellphone service at this time), guarding the front door.

Ah, the "big boys" are here. What perfect timing.

One of the guards of enormous girth stepped forward, halting Estrella in her tracks. "Madre Mia, you're an eyesore," he demeaned. "What do you want, ugly little woman…."

Estrella cut the rude man off, "Go on and insult me all you want. I don't care. I've heard it all before. I'm here to see Señor Padilla."

"He's not seeing anyone, so get the fuck away."

From behind the threatening sentries came the cautioning voice of Gabor, "You should leave! I'll inform Señor Padilla of your visit and that you wish to see him, okay?"

"No, I must see him now!" Estrella fired back.

This fearless small woman wasn't taking *"no"* for an answer.

She dashed past the guards, ran through the door, with the two "armadillos" hot on her heels, yelling profanities. The commotion brought DeLeon to investigate. "What the *mierda* is going on?" When he saw the guards attempting to grab the little person, who was evading their clutches, the ranch owner reacted, irately. "Estrella, what the hell are you doing here? Get back to work! I don't wish to be interrupted. I'm busy."

"You won't be too busy when you hear what I have to say," she brazenly countered.

"*Tócate los cojones*," DeLeon laughed.

The shorter of the two bodyguards laughed, "Yep, the *la enana* (small person) sure got balls, boss."

DeLeon's guests, cartel bosses Charro Morales, Felix Pena, and Miguel Valles, appeared in the hallway. In Estrella's thinking: they were for sure, "shady."

Charro Morales was the first to speak, "Holy shit, I've not seen a dwarf since my mother took me to the circus when I was six."

And that's not going well of late, is it? Lots of your trucks are stopped at the U.S. border, and the contraband is seized by the *policía*. One too many, don't you think?"

His interest piqued, DeLeon spoke for him, "This should be interesting, carry on."

"All I'm asking for is a fair wage if I give you the names of those who rat you out to the border *policía* when they get caught."

Morales and the men alongside him had quizzical looks.

"Come, I would like to talk more," Los Zeta's boss said.

Estrella entered DeLeon's study.

"Sit," her boss said, pointing to an extra-large recliner positioned opposite the now-seated other men. Estrella had to launch herself onto the large leather chair. She felt like a miniature cushion as she sat cross-legged on the recliner.

"Would you like a drink," DeLeon offered.

"Okay," she replied. She took a small swig of the imported Irish whiskey and wished that she hadn't.

Alcohol, mixed with saliva, spewed forth, splashing Charro's expensive shirt. A mortified Estrella spluttered, "I'm so sorry! I don't drink alcohol. It's disgusting. I would like orange juice."

Peals of laughter echoed from the high-beamed ceiling.

Charro Morales broke the laughter. "Now, little woman, let's get down to business. First, I would like you to tell me something that I don't already know."

Getting into heads was her forte.

"Pass me one of your rings, Señor."

Charro wiggled a diamond-encrusted ring from a fat finger and handed it to her.

All eyes now fixed on the fortune-teller and Charro's pinkie ring.

Clasping the ring in a folded hand, Estrella telepathically connected with the wearer. "Your lifespan will be short. You will be betrayed by someone close, a woman you thought you could trust. Two of her sons will die with you in the shootout. Your wife and the rest of your family will be hunted down like wild dogs. But they won't join you in the afterlife."

Charro, a religious man, clicked his tongue, wanting to pass off her dire prophecy as nothing more than a fraud—hocus pocus. But how had she known about his child pants-wetting incident? It was more than mystifying.

One cartel boss, Felix Pena, sneered. "You are as full of crap as a Christmas turkey!"

"I see the future not make it," she bit back.

DeLeon Padilla was quiet, deep in thought. A week or so ago, she had stopped him as he was driving away from the ranch. "Your wife is going to cut your balls off when she finds out you have a mistress!"

He had shrugged it off as nonsense. Now he wasn't so sure. A conversation he had with Hernández popped into his mind: "The little woman I'm sending your way is very "special." She is known here as an "El Sabadora." She has supernatural powers beyond human imagination. Take good care of her, and she will take good care of you."

DeLeon probed his half-brother further, "What do you mean by *supernatural powers*?"

The former priest's comment was, "You'll find out in due course."

His intimate relationship with a Mexican landowner was closely guarded. Only his driver knew of the woman's existence. Or so he thought, until now.

Tension in the study turned into heated arguments.

"She has got to be a fucking witch!"

"I don't believe any of her crap!"

"What if the dwarf is a policía plant?"

"DeLeon, did you check her out before you let her live on your land?" Miguel Valles probed.

Estrella didn't like where this questioning was going. Feeling nervous, she slid off the chair and stated, "I'm leaving now, and it's up to you men to hire me or not!"

Before she could make it from the room, DeLeon's hand firmly latched onto her wrist. "Little woman, tread carefully," he warned. "Go back to the shack and do not repeat to anyone what has transpired in my home."

Her thoughts churned from raw milk to rancid buttermilk. *What have I done? Have I again made bad choices? Should I get the hell away from this ranch?*

Estrella's delicate position, willingness to share her gift of foresight for profit, had not been thought out realistically. Her desire for riches would ultimately bring catastrophic aftermath. One could have never seen coming!

"You reap what you sow!"

Chapter Twenty-Six

Pueblo Viejo, Nuevo Laredo, Mexico

- THE BEGINNING OF AUGUST 2019 -

*"Every negative thing you do or say,
every bad choice you make, sooner or
later comes back around."*
—LUCIA MANN

Twenty-six years had passed, bringing their trials and tribulations. So much had happened in her life up to now.

The aging Estrella, her black hair streaked gray, was no longer the charismatic person, most people wanted in their lives. By jumping into the "lion's den" with dangerous cartel members, who had taken a piece of her all the time, Estrella had abused her spiritual powers for the love of money. It had provided a lifestyle that she could not have imagined: fancy clothes, trips by taxi to hair and manicure salons, and Aminta's private school fees.

It had to end sometime. And it did. Estrella's wakeup call came ten years ago.

At that time, she began experiencing nightmare after nightmare, plagued with earthbound spirits, who had died by cartel violence. The angry shadow beings held her accountable for their brutal deaths. Hadn't she aided their assassins by ratting them out?

Estrella's association with the mob *had* fostered bloodshed and violence—where dead bodies swung from overpasses, their decapitated heads cast along the roadsides, just to secure cartel reigns. Estrella, too, had been their executioner, because she, alone, had handed over their names to these murdering thugs.

The little person's "involvement" wasn't a well-hidden secret.

Word had spread throughout Nuevo Laredo that a *bruja*, an El Salvadoran "witch," was working for the cartels, ratting out moles and gang rivals!

On that late night in 2002, the nightmarish visions continued: The room became unnaturally cold as an ethereal entity loomed over her body.

Estrella was about to encounter a spirit she had not had any communication for a long time. Now, her clairaudient ears tuned to the ominous voice of Kayapa. "Daughter of Waorani blood," she whispered in a low unearthly tone, "You have been misusing your innate gifts of foresight and ancient healing abilities, bestowed upon you by our ageless ones for greed. Granddaughter, you are now cursed with misfortune. You have blood on your hands!"

Estrella heard the growl of a jaguar and *knew* she was in deep trouble.

Shaken by this visitation of doom, Estrella had to get it off her chest. Her only confidant was Gabor, with whom she and Aminta shared a home.

How did this come about?

Back in the year of 1992, after Estrella's "acceptance" into the crime syndicate, she was told by DeLeon Padilla to pack her belongings. She had no idea where she was going until Gabor opened the door of the guesthouse.

"Good morning, Gabor," DeLeon greeted. "I bring you some roommates: Estrella and Aminta. They will be sharing this house with you for the time being."

Gabor was only a renter, so what choice did he have but to accept his boss's orders. The unmarried man didn't know how to "share" his accommodation, let alone have a woman and her child under his roof. Though he had seen them about the ranch from time to time, he had minimal personal contact with them. But he hadn't forgotten the hungry mother and child.

◦⫯◦

In a short time, Estrella and Gabor became more than roommates. But the starry-eyed couple had obstacles to surmount. He loved her with all his heart and wanted their relationship to become intimate, but Estrella had a scar on her heart for life. In her damaged mind, there was no "cookie-cutter" natural way of letting him into her darkest secrets.

Despite the intervening years, the post-rape survivor wounds were still open. She hadn't yet regained her sense of emotional control. Not yet, anyway.

As they spent more time together, Estrella felt a deep love grow inside, one she never felt before for a man. She thought that he could be a good husband. Gabor felt the same way. Did Aminta feel their togetherness? She couldn't have been happier. She adored Gabor.

Life was blissful, but it would not have a fairytale ending.

❦

One day an unexpected visitor arrived at the guesthouse.

"*Cariño* (Darling), there is someone I would like you to meet," Gabor said.

Estrella could have been knocked down by a feather. "I know you. You helped me with my restless daughter on the bus in Ahuachapán."

"That's right," Gabor's biological grandmother returned. "How is she?"

"She's doing fine, still quite rebellious at times, but nothing like she was on the bus that day. Yes, she was the center of attention in those days."

Carmella smiled. "Yes, she was a handful!"

Gabor stepped out of the room to go to work, leaving the women to reminisce.

They chatted about this and that, then Carmella dropped a bombshell when she revealed, "I was once a young prison guard in Ecuador's Pichincha Prison for women…"

The prison's name rang a bell. Estrella was all ears.

Carmella continued, "One of the prisoners was an American woman. Her name was Belicia Godwin, imprisoned for stealing a baby from the Amazon rainforest."

Estrella's jaw dropped. "How do you know this?"

"Just like you, Estrella, I was given special powers at birth. I have come here to warn you that your daughter Aminta will pay the ultimate price for the life that you have chosen."

At a loss for words, Estrella remained calm even though her nerves were somersaulting in shock.

"You of all people should know right from wrong," Carmella declared. "You possess ageless spiritual Amazonian blood. Estrella, you have the innate gifts of foretelling and healing, which you are now abusing for the love of money. You have crossed sacred boundaries with your chosen pathway. It does not sit well with your ancestors in the astral world. Especially not with Kayapa, your grandmother, who weeps for your spirit. She tells me that if you fail to heed this warning, she will forsake you and no longer be your protector."

This encounter with the stark reality left Estrella shaken. With intense emotions, she retorted, "I chose this life to make sure that Aminta never has to suffer extreme poverty as I did. I know what I am doing, and when I have enough money saved, I will walk away from it."

Carmella exhaled sharply. She knew this small, headstrong woman was not going to listen to the sound advice she had given. *So be it!* "My heart hurts for you and for Aminta, who you have cursed by your greed."

Estrella never saw this bearer of ill-omen again.

Some months later, Gabor informed her that Carmella had died in her sleep back home in Guatemala. Estrella wept.

Her tears for the dead woman wouldn't be sufficient to atone for her misguided life path. Everything changed in Estrella's life after Carmella had died. It went from bad to worse. There was no getting away from the dead.

With a reprimanding motion of one finger, Carmella whispered, "I cautioned you to mend your ways. Now an innocent soul will face the consequences of your actions. Oh, how your heart will burn with regret."

Estrella should have taken heed of this and other chilling warnings from beyond the grave! "Descendent of the Amazon, you have to listen to reason, listen to the inner voice telling you what is right or wrong."

As chillingly forecasted, guilt and sorrow would ebb and flow like the mighty Amazon River for the rest of Estrella's life on Earth.

⚭

Shortly before Aminta's thirteenth birthday in 2004, it became apparent that all was not well with the five-foot-five-inch teen. Easily frustrated, she began exhibiting fits of violent aggression when disciplined. Aminta would ball up her fists, and her eyes would enlarge with rage. She had also developed "slowness" in comparison with other children of her age on the Padilla ranch. Alarmingly clusters of scaly warts resembling tree bark appeared, on her hands and feet. Estrella didn't know what to make of this bizarre condition. She reached out to Gabor, "Something is terribly wrong with Aminta."

Gabor's eyes closed tightly. *If only she had listened to my grandmother!*
Gabor had noted Aminta's escalating mood swings but was more

concerned about her bizarre skin disorder that concerned him. "You need to take her to the hospital, get her checked out, and then we must leave this unholy place. We can find somewhere else to live. I can get a job at a restaurant, and support both of you. You and I do not have to work for these crooked people anymore."

Of course, Estrella blatantly ignored her partner's advice as she had done with Carmella and other well-meaning souls. "I'll just work a couple more years, and then we will have enough savings to buy our own home…"

Estrella's sentence abruptly ended when she heard a loud thud coming from a bedroom.

"Call an ambulance!" Estrella screamed.

Later, Estrella faced the doctor after Aminta was rushed to a top hospital. The Russian-born physician introduced himself, "I am Dr. Chertoff. I'm a skin specialist. Your daughter's test results leave no doubt that she has epidermodysplasia verruciformis, known as the Treeman disease. This condition is extremely rare."

His medical explanation was beyond Estrella's comprehension.

"I don't understand," she responded in a puzzled tone.

"Aminta has the autosomal recessive skin disease, which produces tree-bark-looking warts. If the disorder progresses, she will be at a high risk of cancer."

Estrella clamped a hand over her mouth.

"Only a handful of cases exist," Dr. Chertoff stated. "Is there anyone else in your family with this disease?"

In a soft numbed voice, Estrella replied, "Not that I know of." A wishful mother then asked, "Can it be cured?"

"She would have to undergo surgery to remove the bark-like

growths. However, I can't promise that they won't grow back."

Hospital and specialist fees sapped Estrella's savings, leaving her with no alternative but to continue working for the cartel to cover further surgery.

But five more surgeries failed to prevent the "curse" from recurring. Aminta's tree-bark lesions aggressively grew back. The once happy-go-lucky girl, who thought she had a circle of good classmates, soon became the target of their insulting comments:

"Here comes tree wart."

"Do you have tree roots growing out your butt?"

"You better marry a tree, cuz no man is ever going to want you."

◊

At the end of the school year, the Catholic school board sent Estrella a letter.

It is with regret that your daughter Aminta cannot return to school. Aminta does not function at even half the average IQ level required at this school. Her normal speech is impaired, and she often erupts into violent rages toward the other students.

As any parent would, Estrella was livid, but decided that it wasn't the only private school in Nuevo Laredo! Before Estrella could make plans, mushrooming gossip became rampant across town. While waiting in line at the pharmacy, she overheard a parent of one of the students at Aminta's former school say, "God curses the child because of her mother's association with Mexican cartels."

"She's a *rata* (informer). No one is safe around this *bruja*," her companion added.

"I'm glad the school administers have seen right through her."

Estrella paid for Aminta's medicines and exited the store.

As it happens, no school in Laredo was willing to consider enrolling Aminta Lozano. And in the time following Aminta's expulsion, she became withdrawn, veering into impenetrable silence, a muteness not even her devoted mother could break.

Another year passed, the disfigured and mentally-handicapped Aminta needed twenty-four-hour care. Estrella didn't venture far from her child.

The heartbroken mother accepted she was solely to blame, cursed her child, for not heeding the astral warnings to mend her ways, or else!

Aminta was now a *monster,* akin to a grotesque and hideous creature.

After a lot of soul-searching, Estrella's mind became clear. She had to do what she had to do.

❧

DeLeon Padilla did not take well to Estrella's announcement of quitting her "job," and moving away. "I will not be working for you anymore," she announced. "I have got a very sick child and must devote all my time to her now."

"You make a bundle of cash from us!" DeLeon Padilla snapped.

"It's more than enough to pay for a full-time minder. Besides, you will not be off the hook that easily. You are a valuable asset to our business, and no one forced you to join us. You *know* too much about our operations!"

Estrella's blood pressure spiked. "You can't hold me prisoner, Señor Padilla," she scathed. "I am done with giving you the names of people you wish to have killed. What I am doing, I believe, has *cursed* my daughter with an incurable disease."

"What horseshit!" DeLeon retorted. "Nobody forced you to become a *soplón* (snitch). You practically begged to be a participant in our affairs." DeLeon glared menacingly and threatened, "What if I put the word out that you are the *soplón*? You and your disgustingly ugly daughter would be dead in a moment!"

Estrella railed against his intimidation, "Do what you have to do, *bastardo!* I don't care anymore."

"Go then," DeLeon barked. "Pack your bags and leave my ranch! If you repeat a word of what you have seen or here, I can ensure you will not live another day! You'll be a "marked" midget!"

With hot tears of anger streaming down her face, Estrella rushed out of the hacienda and ran head-on into Caitlin Padilla. Several of her shopping bags fell to the ground. "Imbecile, watch where you are going!" she fumed.

"Sorry," Estrella said, and took off like a jackrabbit.

Gabor wasn't at the guesthouse. Estrella grabbed her cellphone. "Where are you?" the voicemail asked.

He didn't text back like he always did.

Strange, Estrella thought.

Aminta, who hadn't spoken a word for some time, broke Estrella's musings, "*Mamacita* is something the matter? You look like you have seen a ghost."

"It's okay, darling," she replied. "We are leaving the ranch today, and I want you to be quiet while I make plans for us, okay?"

Aminta nodded her head. "Is my daddy coming with us?"

Estrella couldn't truthfully answer that question.

The girl loved her substitute father. According to her way of thinking, he *was* her father.

From the time they had moved in with him, Gabor had spent much of his free time settling her into bed, reading bedtime stories, and taking her to parks and, the cinema. They shared the same sweet tooth for rich pastries.

⊙⊱

Leaving her daughter pouting immaturely, Estrella began packing necessities, such as Aminta's medicines and specially-made items to cover her scaly hands and feet. While trying to pack only the stuff that was needed, Estrella felt emotionally at a low web.

Should she go to Gabor's workplace, if that's where he was?

Why had he not replied to her cellphone message?

What if DeLeon had got to him, too? Warned him to break any connection with me, or he might suffer the same fate threatened to me?

Estrella couldn't wait a moment longer. She called a taxi. Their destination was undecided in her haste to escape. As she was stacking luggage in the hallway, she heard a heavy pounding at the front door. It took her off guard. *The taxi couldn't have got here so fast,* her head screamed. Scared out of her wits, she remained still.

The unlocked door swung open and in stepped the most unlikely of guardian angels.

Attired in designer clothing, and adorned in jewelry, stood Caitlin Padilla. "Estrella, are you here?"

"What do you want?" was the sharp reply. "You can tell your husband that I'll be gone as soon as the taxi arrives."

Estrella wasn't expecting the words that followed, "I'm not here on my husband's behalf, I've come to apologize for being so unjust to you, and I'd like you to have this," Caitlin said, handing Estrella a banded money bundle. "It's five thousand dollars to give you and Aminta a new start."

Estrella was speechless. *Why would a woman who had treated her like a rabid dog, now want to help her?*

Of course, there was a reason for her generous offer.

"Before you leave," Caitlin said, "I want you to read my palm and tell me what you see of my future."

Estrella didn't have to read her palm. She already knew what lay in store for the Irish woman. So she came straight out with it. "Señora Padilla, if I were you, I would get as far away from your husband as possible. He has no love for you. He has used you and your wealth and your mob connections to further his riches. Two of his mistresses have born him children. Something he hated about you being barren!"

Caitlin's face lost color. She wanted to say something, but the sound of the taxi horn was her cue. "*Vaya con Dios* (May God be with you)."

"Adiós, Señora. Thank you for the money," Estrella said, adding, "Please listen to me as I wish no harm. For your welfare return to your country of birth, and you will find someone there that will love you for who you are."

For the first time since arriving at the ranch, Estrella saw genuine tears in the woman's eyes. Caitlin removed her wedding ring and diamond engagement. "I want you to have these."

Estrella protested, "I can't take your rings, Señora."

"Yes, you can," Caitlin countered. "They are worth a lot of money. You may need it."

"Thank you so much, Señora. If you see Gabor, please tell him I have my cellphone with me and to call me as soon as he can."

"Will do," she replied.

Estrella and Aminta blew her kisses out of the window of the retreating cab.

The pink and white vehicle sped down the dusty road and out of the Padilla Ranch.

Estrella heaved a sigh of reprieve.

Was she out of the woods? Where was Gabor? Had Estrella's unique memory failed her?

Gabor was in a local dental clinic, waiting to have a bad tooth removed. And he *had* told her about his appointment!

Estrella and Aminta's sudden departure, without a word, would crush Gabor's heart.

Chapter Twenty-Seven

Ahuachapán, El Salvador

- 2005 -

"Life isn't about finding yourself.
Life is about creating yourself."
—GEORGE BERNARD SHAW

Estrella's rushed judgment to go home to El Salvador in 2005, and get away from her involvement with the cartels, came with uncertainty—this lesser of two evils! She had returned to the country of her nightmares, and one of the most dangerous places on Earth.

In this post-war period, El Salvador continued to face problems with poverty, graver than during the war. Roughly half of the six million Salvadorans were unemployed. In this global economic and financial crisis, criminal street gangs sprouted like weeds.

Gang violence was epidemic.

The easiness of obtaining weapons enabled the hourly homicides to proliferate. Fights occurred daily between rival gangs, leading to drive-by shootings, assaults, murders, and other evil crimes. Males and females, ranging from twelve to twenty-five-years old, were willing to fight and die for their gang.

Also, El Salvador faced pollution, trash, and sewage contamination problems due to the lack of environmental laws. Less than three percent of the country remained forested, due to clearing for substantial cultivation of coffee, sugar, and cotton. And back in 1998, Hurricane Mitch and erosion due to deforestation had resulted in disastrous flooding. Many of the country's river systems suffered from toxic waste. Experts feared that at the current rate of destruction, El Salvador would run out of portable drinking water in less than fifteen years.

A theatre of death and disorder surrounded El Salvador and the returnees.

৩৷৩

Estrella chose the border town of Ahuachapán, which held memories of her earlier "escape," to make their new start. Even though she had made a promise never to come back to her country of birth, she reckoned: *Better the devil you know than the devil you don't.*

She bought a rundown home, a steal at three thousand, dollars money from Caitlin's "donation." It was a short distance away from where the bus stopped all those years ago.

The house was of modest size, with a fenced yard, gravel pathway, and a small garden sporting shrubbery and desert cactus. It was by no means the dream home on a rolling acreage she'd once envisioned buying with ill-gotten gains.

But the wow factor for Aminta was a nearby cascading water-fall with clear waters plunging into a rack pool below. Nothing had made Estrella happier than to see the depth of gleeful emotion in her daughter's eyes.

It was the red front door that also delighted Aminta. In her fractured mindset, she could hide behind it without having to wear thick coverings over her hands and feet so her tree-bark hands and feet wouldn't cause shrieks of horror and repulsion.

The afflicted girl never truly realized that she resembled a monster to those who didn't understand nor had ever seen this disorder.

⚬ᶘᴑ

As weeks and months flew by in their new home, Estrella started to feel uneasy. Not with the concern of gang violence that surrounded them, but of someone that she missed dreadfully.

Gabor was never far from Estrella's mind. She hadn't yet heard from him, despite several cellphone messages for him to contact her. It raised unanswerable questions: Why had he not approached her? Had he washed his hands of her?

There *was* a simple answer.

While having his bad tooth extracted, "sticky fingers" had stolen his jacket, containing his cellphone. An angry Gabor drove his truck like a madman. When he arrived back at the guesthouse, the "silence" was bewildering. Had Estrella taken Aminta to the hospital?

He went from room to room, noticing that belongings were gone. Then he saw the note propped up against the bedside drawer.

My darling, Gabor,

I tried to contact you, but couldn't wait a moment longer for your return. We are leaving Mexico because there is a real physical threat to our lives if we remain.

I'll explain all when you contact me.

We love you. Estrella and Aminta

Confounded, Estrella's partner dialed her number from a landline and heard this message: *"El número no está en servicio."* (The telephone number you are calling is not in service.)

He rushed over to the hacienda. "Señor Padilla, do you know what's going on?" he asked, waving Estrella's note in the air. "She left me this letter saying her life was in danger. You know something, don't you?" he confronted accusingly.

DeLeon's face flushed red with fury. "How dare you come into my home with a charge!" he flared. "If she is missing, it has nothing to do with me! Maybe she planned to get away from YOU!"

"She would *never* do that," Gabor responded. "We love each other."

Met with stony silence, the Padilla cook declared, "I'll get to the bottom of this."

That night after finishing his kitchen duties, Gabor headed home to the guesthouse. Lying in wait was a dark figure. A shot rang out, and Gabor fell to the ground.

Later, his naked dead body lay in a deep cow manure pit on the Padilla Ranch.

Gabor was no longer on the Earth.

Gabor, Estrella, and Aminta became ghosts of the past, their names erased from the mouths of bosses and farmworkers.

⚬

In the New Year of 2006, Estrella paced in the garden. She was running short of money. The costly medicines for Aminta were eroding her funds. She had to find work, which was a tall order in these lean days. She considered putting a sign in the window: "*Palmistry Readings*," but decided against it. For a start, no one had the money to "waste," and secondly, she had vowed never to read another's fortune or misfortune again.

That same worrisome day, someone Estrella wasn't expecting stepped back into her life. She noted that he had aged considerably since there last meeting. *What was he doing here?*

Hernández had learned that Ahuachapán had a dwarf resident.

Curiosity killed the cat, and here he was, standing at her gate. "Hello, little woman. It's been some time since we met at the roadside café," the seventy-year-old hailed.

An exhilarated Estrella said, "It's so good to see you. How did you know I was here?"

"I still help those who need help, and one of my "clients," told me about a dwarf that had purchased his house. You will agree with me that there aren't many dwarfs in El Salvador, so I just put two and two together."

"Come in," Estrella said, gesturing at the red door.

"Thank you," Hernández replied. "We have catching up to do."

"Yes, we have," Estrella agreed. "Would you like a glass of "fire-water"?

"That would be most welcome," the dry-mouthed man accepted.

Since returning home, Estrella had taken to drinking excessively. Her tipple was "fire-water"—*aguardiente*, an illicitly distilled drink made from sugarcane that cost about fifty cents a bottle. She didn't plan on getting drunk with the former priest, but alcohol loosened her lips, and she spilled out everything that had happened since he had handed her the fake documents all those years ago.

Hernández listened intently without interruption, and then with compassion written in his wrinkled features, the former priest took hold of Estrella's quivering hands. "Where is your daughter?" he asked.

"She's in the back room. She won't come out unless I call her."

"Please call her out. I would like to see her affliction for myself."

Hernández's face was unreadable when Aminta, hands hidden behind her back, walked toward him.

"Darling," Estrella motioned. "This is Señor Hernández. He's our good friend."

Aminta frowned. There were no friends in her life except her mother. In a childlike voice, she asked, "Can you make this?" She swung her heavy, distorted hands into view. "Go away?"

Without thought, Hernández blurted, "Holy mother of God!"

Before Estrella could counteract his astonished outcry, Aminta stomped out of the room, back to the safety of her bedroom, sobbing.

"Poor child," Hernández uttered. "I'm sorry, Estrella, I should have been considerate. What is this disorder as I have never seen anything like it?"

Estrella gave the specialist's diagnosis, then her own, "I'm to blame for her condition because I've exploited my spiritual gifts for money."

Hernández didn't give it credibility. "Though I have long left the Catholic Church, Estrella, and its teachings, I am still a disbeliever when it comes to supernatural events."

In the back of this former's priest's mind was a contrary thought: *But then who am I to say what is real and what is not?*

Estrella felt that the time had come to "open" his fixed mindset. "I *know* the reason why you left the church, and it sickens me. But I will not sit in judgment. That will be up to your God..."

Hernández interrupted doubtfully, "You don't know anything!"

"Well then, you are about to be converted," Estrella responded. "Behind you stands a small shadow figure, a twelve-year-old boy. He tells me his name is Alejandro and that you molested him when he was ten. He informs me that he's not the only boy that you defiled in the vestry. But he is now with God, and has forgiven you, he says."

Hernández's face was ashen.

The medium was not done. "One of your victims told his mother, who immediately filed a complaint with the bishop, who, in turn, advised her not to report your vile behavior to the police. He would handle it. And the bishop did just that. He relieved you of your priestly duties. Correct? Also, your superior demanded that you leave San Salvador for good. Correct?"

The smug "*gotcha!*" expression on Estrella's face was priceless.

The wide-eyed Hernández was blown away by her knowledge. How could she have known these shameful secrets? There was little doubt now that there was *something* beyond the rote of the Catholic Church's stance to clairvoyance phenomena.

Hernández resignedly accepted, "Yes, I'm a fallen man. But I have not hurt another innocent soul by my sickness since leaving the priesthood. I did not want to become a priest, but my mother forced me into it. She knew as all mothers do that I was "different" attracted to males. My God-fearing mother believed the priesthood would cure my homosexual tendencies. Well, it didn't. I'm a changed man. I sought God's forgiveness and have dedicated my remaining years on Earth to atone by helping others, even if such assistance is illegal."

"I know you are telling the truth," Estrella said. "Aminta and I could not have gotten out of El Salvador without you. We owe you our lives, so let's move past this."

Hernández's discomfort decreased. His action took Estrella by surprise.

He rose from his chair and warmly hugged her. "If there is anything I can do for you all you need is to ask."

Estrella grabbed this opportunity, "Do you know someone who will hire a dwarf? I don't mean a circus recruiter," she laughed. "You see, I'm running out of money, and will shortly not be able to afford Aminta's costly medicines or the upkeep of this house."

The former priest gave it thought before saying, "Yes, I do know someone, who could offer you a job, but it's *risky*," he emphasized, averting her prying eyes. "I don't know if my contact will accept you, but I will give it my best shot."

"Explain," Estrella insisted.

"I will have to speak to him first."

Mystery hung in the air.

Chapter Twenty-Eight

Crossing Machiavellian Boundaries

- 2006–2018 -

"There is nothing nobler than risking your own life for your child."
—Lucia Mann

After Hernández departed, Estrella couldn't sleep. Her thoughts were troubled about the potential "work" proposal and what it might involve. Her thoughts were that—she just couldn't risk further danger to herself and Aminta.

That night, mustering all of her psychic energy, she had tried to *see* a clear picture butt to no avail. However, about one thing, she was sure. If taken on, by whomever, she sensed it was likely equally as dangerous as her former employment. Was she prepared to "risk" everything for the sake of money once more? What would happen to her sick child if the "work" was risky? Suppose she was to lose her life? Would an orphanage refuse to accept her child because she was a freak of nature? Estrella's mother, Analena, had told horror stories about her own life in an orphanage.

That last thought spurred her into action.

She made a premature telephone call. "Okay, Señor Hernández, tell your contact that I will undergo whatever, but only on one condition."

"I'm listening."

"If something should happen to me, promise me that Aminta will never end up in an orphanage or a mental asylum."

"I do promise," Hernández avowed. "Are you certain about this, Estrella?"

"I don't have much choice, do I?" she answered. "If I don't do whatever is in store for me, we will starve. I just can't let that happen."

"Then, I will see you tomorrow morning."

⚬⟋⟍⚬

Hernández turned up bright and early.

The anxious Estrella finally learned about her new employment. She wasn't shocked but had concerns. "As I will be traveling to and from El Salvador, could you find someone to care for Aminta while I'm gone?"

"I'm one step in front of you, little woman! She's a former nun and a retired mental-health nurse."

"Did you tell her my daughter has treeman disorder?"

"Yes, I did. Sister Margarita has worked with lepers. I don't think Aminta's condition will concern her in the slightest. I've known Margarita for years. She's a kind, caring person. I believe

Aminta will be very comfortable with her."

To hear this was a significant weight off Estrella's mind. Aminta wasn't a "normal" babysitting project. This teenager had to be handfed, changed regularly, and her immature mind continuously occupied. If Estrella were too tired to read Aminta a bedtime story, she would scream her lungs out until her mother complied!

Hernández broke her thoughts. "Now, I have other matters to attend to, but I will return later."

That evening, the disgraced priest appeared with someone who took Estrella entirely by surprise.

"I'd like you to meet Carlito Fuentes, your new boss," Hernández said, smiling.

Estrella couldn't take her eyes off this mysterious person with similar characteristics to her own. The man was of her height and age. In Estrella's imagination, he had just stepped out of the Wizard of Oz. She had not seen another LP (little person) since leaving Mexico, and not up this close.

The well-dressed Carlito was pleasing to her eyes. What a handsome fellow was her immediate thought. He, too, was spontaneously drawn to her. In a baritone voice, the American-born Carlito greeted Estrella, "*Mucho gusto* (Pleased to meet you.)"

She immediately felt her cheeks start to redden after his firm handshake, not to mention the flurry of dancing butterflies in her stomach. "*Mucho gusto,*" she returned, hoping flushed cheeks didn't give her away.

With the pleasant aroma of his aftershave wafting in the air, the three sat at the table. Hernández spoke first, "Estrella, Carlito is going to run the assignment with you, as I have to meet with someone else. I'll be back shortly."

Estrella nodded. To be left alone with a man she thought was cute was romantically exciting. Even though her relationship with Gabor was terrific, she had never felt this "fuzzy" for the opposite sex, ever!

Carlito began, "What I'm about to tell you is highly confidential," the well-educated Harvard graduate stated.

"Of course," Estrella answered. "Hernández has already informed me."

Estrella listened without interruption while Carlos unveiled the "work" to be carried out in utmost secrecy.

Estrella was utterly amazed. Never in her wildest dreams could she have imagined being a part of this kind of operation. And yes, this first assignment *was*, indeed, risky. However, the thought of getting a good paycheck, and to get out of poverty, was all that it took.

Estrella cooperatively signed the Confidentiality Agreement, a legal document that protected sensitive information from being revealed. Carlito then placed the agreement in his briefcase. "Do you have any questions?"

Of course, questions flooded and one of priority. "How did you become an undercover CIA agent? And why?"

"Actually, what I do is mundane. My job is to provide Intel, such as to gather, analyze, and pass on intelligence on foreign countries to U.S. heads of security. I'm not sure you are aware that, once more, the current political landscape here in El Salvador is becoming very unstable like it was before the civil war. So intelligence findings are crucial."

Estrella had heard rumors to this effect but hadn't given it much thought.

Carlito continued, "I've been monitoring radio and television broadcasts, translating what's being said and written. I look for information that's related to a possible threat to the U.S. as the White House believes the former guerilla group, FMLN, is trying to regain power. America needs assurance that El Salvador's leftist movement does not become a threat in the future."

Cognizance sparked Estrella's reaction. "So, what you are telling me is that you are a spy, right?"

"In a nutshell, yes," he replied. "The CIA's psychological trick is to prevent threats by gathering Intel, so that's where I come in."

Carlito retrieved a file that was stamped CLASSIFIED from his briefcase and handed her the top-secret file. "You are to memorize the contents, then burn the file."

With work put aside, the two LP's discussed their backgrounds. Carlito had already obtained certain background information on his recruit, but not as much as he would like.

Estrella felt so comfortable in his presence, an immediate "bonding" of trust unwrapped.

She recapitulated her Amazonian roots, her deceased parents, the abduction of her foster brothers, and the arson. But Estrella couldn't bring herself to disclose her sexual violation, not just yet. Or her "involvement" with the guerrilla fighters and she also deliberately omitted disclosure of her clairvoyant capabilities that had given her nothing but trouble. She didn't wish to spoil their getting to know each other on a more relaxed level.

Carlito also felt at ease in her company. He spoke of his deceased Mexican-born average-sized mother and his father and confided, "Forty-five years ago, my mother met and fell in love with an American airman. When she became pregnant, they married and moved to the U.S., but it wasn't to be a happily ever after ending for my poor mother. When I was born, my father accused my mother of messing around."

Estrella detected the bitterness in his voice. "That's awful," she sympathized.

"My father's idiotic reasoning was that there were no dwarfs on his side of the family, so in other words, she must have slept with someone else…"

Estrella interrupted, "Oh, that's horrible. My father *never* questioned my mother. Neither of my parents had any dwarfs in their ancestry that they knew of either."

Carlito continued, "As a single parent, my mother dedicated her life to me, I being her only child. She never remarried and worked three jobs to put me through school, college, and then university. I graduated in Political Science and was recruited by the CIA shortly after. I've been working as an operative for many years now."

Estrella's mind became deluged and needed—answers. "You said that your mother was dead. What happened to her?"

The high-ranking officer responded with sadness, "I knew she was unhappy in the U.S., so after I had graduated, I gave my mother options. I told her she could come and live with me in my apartment, or I could buy her a home. She preferred to return to her country of birth to live out her days on earth, she said. I told her it was out of the question because Nuevo Laredo was way too dangerous. It was at that time the murder capital of the world."

Estrella felt icy chills run down her spine at his mention of the place that she had fled. Without giving her feelings away, she gazed at the man who continued to fascinate her.

"I did oblige her wish. I bought her a nice house in Mexico and visited her as often as I could. She died there two years ago from pancreatic cancer."

"I am truly sorry to hear that," Estrella said. "What about your father?"

Carlito's features twisted with repugnance. "I learned that he had remarried, and I now have five half-siblings. I notified him of my mother's death, and he didn't respond. So, I want nothing to do with him. As far as I'm concerned, he is dead as well."

This bitterness towards his father wasn't easily dismissed. Although she didn't want to admit it, her own father's abrupt exit from her life had left pain in Estrella's heart. But more pressing questions required answers. "Are you married? Do you have children?"

Carlito smiled. "No, I'm not married. I don't have any children that I know of," he ended with a twinkle in his eyes.

"What about you? Hernández told me you have a teenage daughter. Is she here with you in El Salvador?"

"Yes, she's here with me. Her name is Aminta. I named her after Archbishop Romero's deceased infant sister."

"May I meet her?" Carlito asked.

The memory of the Hernández's introduction caused Estrella to rethink. She didn't want Aminta to encounter another "*Holy Mother of God*" scenario. Protectively she replied, "Aminta is in the back bedroom, watching television. She is timid, so maybe another day, okay?"

They parted company.

Estrella had pleasant dreams that night.

So did Carlito. He had gone through failed relationships with average-sized women, but none had captivated him, and he longed to be with someone of his stature.

⚜

The "pretend" married couple, Señor and Señora *Lopez*, arrived by taxi at El Salvador International Airport. Estrella was thrilled to be holding her seeming husband's hand. She was not so enthusiastic about the USB "flash drive" sewn into the padding of her bra. Before entering the airport, Carlito had demonstrated how to maintain a calm demeanor while going through customs.

"I'm already a pro at that," Estrella had returned laughingly. "I've crossed more borders with false identification than you have had hot dinners."

"You wanna bet?" Carlito had grinned.

Now, as he walked beside her, he couldn't help but admire his new partner. She was everything he liked in a woman—witty, strong-minded, independent, extremely intelligent, and attractive in his eyes. But he reminded himself—his work came before any relationships. He did, however, wish that one day they would be more than just working partners.

Estrella read his mind! Her heart was beating with such rapture, a joy never felt before, as they strolled up to Passport Control, with their Salvadoran passports. There was no denying that Hernández was an expert forger.

Five hours later, the couple arrived at LAX (Los Angeles International Airport.)

"What is the purpose of your visit?" they were queried.

"We have an appointment at UCLA Medical Centre with a skin disorder specialist," Carlito replied. "Our daughter has treeman syndrome," he added, handing over a photograph of Aminta. The officer winced at the picture, promptly stamped their passports, and waved them through.

Outside, Estrella heaved a sigh of: "*thank God that's over.*"

෨෴

Booked into the La Quinta Inn & Suites, she tore open the bra padding and gave Carlito the flash drive. He put the memory stick into his pants pocket, and then made a cellphone call using a "burner," a disposable pre-paid cellphone. When the conversation ended, he turned to Estrella. "Order whatever you like from room service, because I've no idea how long I'll be gone. See you later, *wife*. You did well," he genuinely praised.

Estrella beamed. She was thrilled to be his co-conspirator partner.

That same night, after a few cocktails, they kissed and cuddled. Later, for the first time in her entire life, Estrella experienced intimacy without the dark shadow of sexual violation.

It was a night she would never forget. Now she had a "connection." She happily mused: *Life doesn't get much better.*

In 2009, after the presidential elections, the FMLN had achieved a milestone in their campaign. In the polls, sixty percent of Salvadorans voted for the leftist and former journalist Mauricio Funes, who took over as president, together with Salvador Sanchez Ceren as his vice president. The guerilla group now had real power for the first time since the end of the war in 1992.

Estrella revealed to the love of her life her involvement with the FMLN rebels and then, her darkest secret—the violation and the abduction of her brothers that had led her to the rebel fighters. Carlito held her tightly. It was as if he was telling her to put those events into the trash bin forever.

And finally, that is what the unburdened little woman did.

Now they had no more secrets between them.

Or so she thought!

Four years later, after many successful "assignments" around the world, Carlito and Estrella were formally married in San Diego. Her forged documents never came under the radar!

One year later, Estrella received a permanent residency status from the U.S. government in gratitude for her undercover work. In this same year, she returned to El Salvador to get her daughter, who had remained at the Ahuachapán residence in the care of the former nun.

After arriving in the U.S., Aminta underwent further surgery, but the "curse" relentlessly returned. It was as if La Mancha Mama, the sacred tree spirit, had abandoned her protection for good.

⚬

Now, at age forty-seven, Estrella opted out of her "arrangement" with Carlito. The stay-at-home mom dedicated every day to caring for the now twenty-two-year-old Aminta, whose handicapped needs had escalated.

No longer able to walk unaided, Estrella bought Aminta a wheelchair and took her disabled daughter out of the house as often as she could manage. There were days that Estrella needed to calm the mentally-challenged Aminta, who had not taken to her new stepfather. Estrella had reproached, "He is good to us both. Please show him at least some respect, and stop calling him *Gabor*. You know he is not Gabor."

Aminta bit back, "I know things, Mamacita, which you don't! He is *not* a good man."

Estrella chose to ignore her daughter's allegation. Was Aminta gifted with the prophetic vision now denied to her mother?

⚬

One day, Carlito surprised his wife with a wheelchair-accessible SUV, with a custom driver's seat and multi-function controls integrated into the steering wheel. He taught Estrella how to drive. She passed the driving test and received her first-ever license. From that day on, Estrella drove Aminta to parks, restaurants, malls, and hair salons just to make her child feel like a "normal" person.

Alas, this heavenly contented life was to have an unforeseen tragic end.

On February 11, 2018, a domestic Russian flight from Moscow to Orsk failed to land as scheduled. It seemed that the aircraft had crashed only six minutes into its flight. All seventy-one passengers and the pilot and co-pilot died. Carlito was one of these seventy-one victims.

When Estrella learned of her husband's death, she broke down.

In the time they had been together, Estrella knew better than to ask questions about his whereabouts when he announced that he was going "Dark," the term used for out of reach. On this particular occasion, Carlito had, however, afforded some information to his wife. "I'm off to Europe, and I'll be back in a week or so."

ঔ

Now, after the fatal crash, it didn't make sense to Estrella, why had her husband misled her? Why he had he kept this Moscow, trip from her was puzzling. From the time they had legally married, she honestly believed that there were *no* secrets between them. She had not chosen to use her mind-reading "gift" with Carlito. She had put telepathy out to pasture.

ঔ

After the private funeral, attended only by a few close colleagues, Estrella descended into a very dark depression. She fell to the bottom of the pit, taking succor by using alcohol, antidepressants, and the odd smoke of marijuana.

Flying high on this Friday, Estrella was not on the planet when the lawyer read Carlito's Will and Testament.

WILL OF CARLITO LEONEL FUENTES

1. This is my Will, and it replaces earlier Wills that I have made.
2. In my Will,

    (a) I leave my wife a 2.39-acre property in Laredo, Mexico.

    (b) I appoint my wife Estrella Lozano Fuentes as the Executor of my Will and Trustee of my estate...."

The lawyer's words were a blur. But the widow did apprehend the clause about the home that Carlito owned (the house bought for his mother) in Nuevo Laredo, Mexico.

Estrella left the lawyer's office with one decisive action in mind. She didn't want to stay in her present home. It held too many fond memories. There was no longer anything to keep her in the U.S.

On the way home, Estrella's thoughts ranged:

Should she sell up and return to El Salvador? Out of the question, her brain answered. Should she relocate back to Mexico? Again out of the question!

During the coming days, Estrella was to learn that finances weren't as rosy as she had assumed. She had received a default notice in the mail. The mortgage on the house hadn't been paid in three months, and the bank was threatening foreclosure. The SUV, Carlos' gift, had nine repayments outstanding. The credit card debt was also significant.

Estrella was perplexed. How was this even possible? She thought they were well-off. Carlos' salary was more than two hundred three thousand US dollars per year.

Estrella drove to the bank.

There, to her chagrin, their joint account contained only three hundred US dollars. Where had all the money gone?

Back at the house, using Carlito's password, Estrella signed onto his computer. What she discovered was the stuff of fiction writers! The angry woman threw the laptop onto the floor. In a tail-spin, Estrella thought that she had known her significant other. Wrong! Carlito was a fraud, a liar! His double life was revealed in hundreds of emails and text messages.

It transpired that Carlito was guilty of unprosecuted bigamy. He had married another woman, a second wife and co-worker twenty years younger, had two sons, aged four and six with her, and an upscale house, and a pet dog.

Estrella couldn't believe it! She didn't even *want* to consider it! What bugged her was why had she not *seen* this infidelity? She was so good at "reading" other people. How could her telepathic sense have been so out of touch?

Estrella believed she had that answer.

She was barred—no spiritual access because she had abused her innate, inherited gifts. What baffled her was how her husband had managed to pull off this deception, keeping the charade going for so long. Obviously, he had not taken *their* marriage vows to heart!

Now, a spurned Estrella wanted to satisfy humiliation with a retaliatory action—email the *other* woman, Lilian Thompson. "Did you know he was married? And, if so, did you care? Well, your *husband* is dead. There will be no more paychecks!"

Something at the back of Estrella's mind remained unanswered. Did Lilian *know* about Carlito's death? As far as Estrella was aware, there had been no public obituary, a decision made by his superiors. And if the CIA had known about their operative's "other" woman, had she so been informed. Had Lilian told her children that their father wasn't coming home again?

Estrella's compassionate heart now ached for this "other" family. These feelings of tenderness switch didn't last on for long. Everyone has their breaking point, and this was it for Estrella.

In angry reprisal, she ripped up all of the "happier-times" photographs and disposed of his clothing, personal toiletry items, and his laptop, into a dumpster.

After hours of "memorable" obliteration, nothing remained in their home that could have linked them together as spouses.

That day, and with a heavy heart, Estrella called an international removal company.

Chapter Twenty-Nine

Nuevo Laredo, Mexico

- 2018 -

*"Violent death erases more than
the semblance of life."*
—P.D. JAMES

Before making that telephone call, Estrella had not envisioned moving back to Mexico, to this place of bad memories *and* possible danger. However, in her troubled mind, what was worse—being homeless in the U.S. with no money? She was darn sure fast-food chains wouldn't be hiring a dwarf any time soon. She could not reach up to counters without a stool or carry more than one plate of food at a time. Her hands were now so arthritic that she could hardly brush her hair, let alone Aminta's, without feeling discomfort. To add to woes, the home she had lovingly shared with a man she thought would never have betrayed her *was* in foreclosure. The electricity was cut off, and the food supplies were dwindling.

Carlito's blatant indifference towards the wellbeing of *this* family was unfathomable. She became livid when she found that his pension plan death benefits went to Lilian Thompson. All Estrella had received was three hundred dollars in cash and a pile of debts that, according to the lawyer, she was now responsible for paying. Estrella was damned if she was going to fork out the mounting debts and unpaid taxes Carlito had incurred during their marriage. Not being unable to provide the basic needs for her sick daughter had confirmed Estrella's decision to return to Mexico. After all, she was legally entitled to the fully paid residence, a 2.39-acre property once owned by his mother. Estrella's thinking could provide income from food crops.

Before she made up her mind to return to Mexico, robbing a bank had been a fleeting option. With her identifiable stature, this would have been hilarious!

⊂┃⊃

Now, in Mexico, Estrella was thrilled with the cozy, ready to a move-in farmhouse located in Los Indios, a small border town overlooking the Rio Grande, near San Benito.

The farmhouse had three bedrooms, two bathrooms, and a fair-sized kitchen. Attached to the home was a double garage. As Estrella wheeled her up to the house, Aminta's face lit up with delight when she saw the LED-lit fountain, its lion's head spouting water. The new homeowner was happy to see her daughter so delighted.

It had been taxing for her to take Aminta on the long journey from California to Mexico. However, Estrella had felt that Aminta would relish the quiet of this secluded home, far removed from the hustle of the fast-paced American life, and somewhat removed from the Padilla Ranch. A musing did cross Estrella's mind. What if DeLeon and his cronies discovered she had returned? Would they come after her?

She planned to keep a low profile.

⁙

In a happy place, Estrella kicked her depression habits—alcohol, prescription medicines, and weed. Her physical health and mental state improved. After purchasing quality seeds, she planted beans, squash, and tomatoes. It was backbreaking toil for a single person, but the rewards paid off.

After harvesting, Estrella had made good money at the local market, earning enough to put adequate food on the table and buy Aminta's medicines, which were half the price she'd paid back in the U.S.

And life at the farmhouse went happily on.

⁙

In August 2019, Estrella needed to make a trip to the pharmacy. She headed for Aminta's bedroom. "Darling, I'm just popping out to buy milk, and pick up your medicines. Stay in your bedroom and watch television. I won't be long and don't open the door to *anyone*, okay?"

Head nodding, Aminta promised to obey her mother's instructions.

At 3:00 p.m., Estrella parked the 1960's Volkswagen Beetle in the pharmacy parking lot. As she was exiting the vehicle, a tall slim man, wearing a black hoodie low over his face, black pants, and sneakers, approached her. "Have you got a cigarette?"

"Sorry, I don't smoke."

"I thought it was you," he snarled in a gravelly voice. "How could I *ever* forget?" He pulled out a hunting knife and threatened, "If you scream or try to escape, I will kill you."

Every muscle in Estrella's being screamed at her to take flight, but her petrified body remained frozen. Having a weapon directed at her brought back horrific memories. She could still feel the cold steel of her rapist's gun pressed against her left temple.

At around 3:26 p.m., in broad daylight, Loco (Julio Olivares) abducted Estrella. Grabbing her, he threw her into the passenger seat of a red pickup truck parked alongside her Volkswagen. "Get on the floor," he ordered. "If you move an inch, I'll cut your throat."

Estrella was so scared, hardly breathing at all. She knew *him*. Those same dead eyeballs had confronted her at the Guatemalan border all those years ago. He was now the controller of her fate.

Her abductor's heavy foot on the accelerator and the knife visible on his lap, the truck sped away.

The heavily-tattooed MS-13 gang member had much to say to his doubled-up captive under the dashboard. "My mother told me all about you and the false accusation that you made against my father. Your rape claim is a load of shit! My father was a religious man. He wouldn't have done this to you or anyone else."

Her insides quivering, Estrella remained silent, as the manic Loco raved on, "After the war, a Masahaut priest and a hospital doctor reported your *so-called* rape to the police. They said they had evidence! My father protested that he had not raped anyone." Loco's eyes flashed with hatred as they locked onto Estrella's wide eyes. "Your fuckin' lies killed my father. He hung himself while awaiting trial! His suicide sent my mother into madness. You are going to get what's coming to you, you lying bitch!"

Estrella pleaded, "Please, I have a very sick daughter who could be your half-sibling…"

The back of Loco's hand hit her hard in the face. "*Cállate* (Shut up) lying bitch."

Estrella wasn't going to give up. "If I don't return home, my crippled daughter is going to die because she can't feed herself."

This time, Loco's clenched fist struck Estrella's nose. The cracking of her nasal bone echoed audibly. Her eyes began to water, and blood poured from her nostrils. Estrella passed out.

When consciousness finally returned, Loco's hostage found herself bound with ropes to a wooden pillar. Swollen half-closed eyes took in the unfamiliar surroundings.

Above the cement floor, large metal hooks hung from rotting beams. To the side of Estrella, a refrigerated truck had been stripped bare, right down to the metal chassis. On one wall, an old sign hung: **PLANTA EMPACADORA Y MATADERO** (Packing Plant & Abattoir).

Estrella's nightmarish prison was an abandoned slaughterhouse!

Her abductor was missing from the premises.

Though terrified, Estrella went into escape mode, but the rope restraints held. She sobbed, not for herself, but for Aminta, who would by now be frantic. The captive had only one option left. "Kayapa, I need your help. I'm asking you to please forgive me for breaking the rules of the ancient spiritual practices bestowed on me. I've been such an idiot! But I am still a human, and Aminta and I are going to die if you don't help us. Please, please, Kayapa, hear me!"

Estrella felt the sudden change of temperature, then the comforting feeling that engulfed her shivering body. "Kayapa, you have heard me, thank you. Help me escape before that monster returns." Through peripheral vision, she observed the shadow figure floating towards her. The unearthly message was clear, but not from whom she thought it to be. "Granddaughter of my daughter, Kayapa, you carry the blood of our ancient warriors. Waorani only spills the blood of intruders who threaten our way of life," the chieftain stated. "Your ancestors are displeased because there is blood on your hands, indirectly handed over the lives of others for material gain. That is why the mysteries of your mind gifts were lost, taken from you the moment you entered that dark way of life. Your wrongdoings must be avenged to appease our gods. You will join us shortly..."

The ethereal voice faded away. Estrella wept.

Sensing that death was near, Estrella began to channel all the spiritual energy she could muster to connect to the "other" invisible dimension.

"I'm not afraid to die," she stated. "I cannot change the past and apologize for the actions that I soulfully regret. Please grant me a last wish and direct someone, a living person, to care for my child who cannot manage for herself."

An icy temperature once more surrounded her. Had her plea been received seriously?

With her head slumped forward, Estrella pondered: What had been her purpose in life? To heal others seeking physical and spiritual guidance. She had failed the test!

But the little person didn't deserve the brutality that would soon become her reality.

⚬⟊⟀

Loco, with a fixed glare of madness, returned with two of his gang members. Reeking of hard liquor and marijuana, and with dilated pupils from the intake of other illicit drugs, the men with unhinged minds gathered around Estrella. With the blackest of hearts, they stripped her naked. She was assaulted, beaten, and then stabbed multiple times in the abdomen, chest, neck, and head. Before her mortal life receded, like the tide, she shot her perpetrators a look of purest hatred, then uttered her final words, "Forgive me, my darling, Aminta. I love you. I'll be waiting for you on the other side, a happier place for you and me."

Estrella's lifeless body was thrown into the back of a pickup truck and covered with a dirty tarp and then, thrown into the Rio Grande like trash for Agents Dalton and Rivas to discover.

⚬⟊⟀

Back at the farmhouse, Aminta wrapped a plastic tablecloth around herself, to conceal soiled pajamas then awkwardly she manipulated her cumbersome body into the motorized, mouth-controlled wheelchair. Aminta sued tongue movements transmitted to the onboard computer to bravely venture outside the home, something not done before without her mother being present. She squinted in the bright morning sun. The raucous *caw-caw* of crows gathered atop a nearby tree frightened her. A squawk similar to the crow's calls exploded from her mouth, and the birds hit the sky. Aminta was exiting the farmhouse driveway, not knowing where to go. She spotted a truck heading towards her. The driver of the vehicle turned to his passenger, "Are you sure we are at the right place?" Loco queried.

"Yes, it *is* the right place. I found the bitch's passport and driving license in her vehicle before I torched the Beetle," his passenger stated, rechecking the documents held in his hand.

The red pickup truck came to a screeching halt. The vehicle occupants had never seen anything like it.

Revulsion curdled Loco's stomach as he stood in front of Aminta's wheelchair. "*Que chingado!* (What the fuck!) You *are* a monster, not a human! What rock did you crawl out from under, or should I say dead tree?"

His passenger added his piece, "Better still, who let you out of the zoo?"

"You gotta be Frankenstein's sister, escaped from a mad scientist's experiment lab," Loco uttered. "You are most *definitely* not of my father's blood!"

Their derogatory comments didn't make any sense to the

simple-minded Aminta. Hadn't Estrella told her that she was "special" and beautiful?

She queried, "Have you seen my mother?"

"We sure have," Loco sneered.

"Can you take me to her—?"

She didn't see it coming.

The rock struck her temple hard, driving shattered bones into her brain. The injured girl fell out of her wheelchair, collapsing on the dirt driveway. The thugs looked at each other. "Let's get the fuck out of here," urged Loco's partner in crime.

The stolen pickup truck sped down the driveway, like a bat out of Hell.

With hemorrhaging cutting off the oxygen to her brain, Aminta's organs began failing, until finally, she exhaled the last breath that carried but one word, "Mamacita."

Sometime later, the sounds of sirens disturbed the quiet of the farmhouse driveway.

A mother's love is the most powerful emotion in the world!

In the rear of the ambulance, an otherworldly Mamacita cradled her daughter's bloodied head. Aminta's human eyes forever closed to the living, a silent voice from beyond whispered, *"Mamacita, you came back."*

"Yes, my darling. I'm here. I'll never leave you again. Look, daughter, look who is here. Your great-grandmother, Kayapa, and your grandmother, Analena and all our passed-over family, have their arms out, waiting for us to join them."

An eerie chill permeated the ambulance compartment. The souls of the dead were now all reunited.

Loco had taken Estrella's and Aminta's mortal lives, but not their immortal spirits that entered an astral dimension together, never to be parted.

Was Aminta indeed *cursed* from birth? Or was she just a mindless child cruelly labeled?

Would Estrella and Aminta's immortal soul's return to reincarnate, become "Earth Angels" for others who lose their moral ways and walk down the wrong paths? Perhaps!

Chapter Thirty

Arizona

- DECEMBER 2019 -

*"Sooner or later, karmic payback will come after you,
send you the revenge deserved. Be prepared to pay
the ultimate price for the evil done to another."*
—LUCIA MANN

Before Christmas of this year, a local drug bust produced a much-awaited "snitch" incarcerated at the Red Rock Correction Facility in Arizona.

Naturally, a skeptic by nature, the paranoid Sandoval, was guarded. From longstanding experience, he had learned never to trust informers, trying to save their hides, especially those with ulterior motives like: "I'll tell you everything I know for a reduced prison sentence."

What had he to lose, after all these years?

But why had the convicted drug trafficker asked to speak to him personally was baffling as Sandoval was long retired and residing in Texas!

"Do you accept this collect call from an inmate, Santiago Wilfredo?"

"Yes." Detective Sandoval said to the caller, "I'm all ears."

"Loco, Julio Olivares, is going by the name of Mario Montoya," Carlos, an MS-13 gang member, reported. "He is using a fake U.S. green card and living in Yuma with his pregnant girlfriend."

"How do you know this?" Sandoval queried in a restrained tone.

"I was his cellmate for two years."

"What was his arrest charge?" Sandoval asked.

"According to Loco, he got pulled over in a routine traffic stop, and the cop got "wacky" on him when he saw his gang tattoos. One thing led to another, and Loco punched a cop in the mouth. He got five years. With good behavior, he has served two. He was released a couple of days ago."

"And?" Sandoval pushed.

"While he was my cellmate, I was surprised to learn that we were Salvadorēnos, and believe it or not we were on the same plane being deported back to El Salvador."

"You say that you were friends. Well in my book friends don't rat each other out. So why are you rolling over on your *friend*?"

"I have to do what's right. What Loco told me sickened me to my stomach," was the reply.

Still wary Sandoval pressed on, "Carry on."

"Loco told me that back in 1994 he had murdered an old man in Laredo, Texas. And later that he strangled and stabbed a dwarf, whom he hated with a passion. He also told me that he bashed in the head of her daughter, a freaky-looking girl in a wheelchair."

Sandoval's back straightened. *Old man! Dwarf and freaky-looking girl!*

"Man, I'm a hardened criminal, in this shithole for drug smuggling, but killing a helpless, disabled girl is a no-no in my world. But let me tell you, you are going to have your work cut out for you because Loco is not dumb, he is criminally sophisticated. Like I have said, he told me he broke into a home in Texas, killed a senior, stole his wallet and jewelry, and evaded capture. The dwarf woman he killed was from El Salvador. Loco said he drove his truck with her dead body covered with a tarp and dumped her in the Rio Grande."

Credibility hit home:

The informer could not have *known* these precise details: they were not released to the press. He had promised the Rivas family back in 1994 that one day he would get the bastard who killed Arnoldo. The thought of finally capturing the killer of *three* people spurred him into immediate action. "Are you willing to take a polygraph?"

"Yup," was Santiago's immediate reply. "But, I want to trade for a reduced sentence."

The informer passed the test. "There is no deception," stated the polygraph expert.

Sandoval put the wheels in motion and did a follow-up investigation at his end. Then he placed a call to the Deputy Sheriff in Yuma.

Twenty-four hours later, Sandoval arrived at Yuma International Airport. Waiting for him was Special Agent Holder, who was earlier briefed.

Sandoval had couriered the Rivas cold case file documents to Holder ahead of his arrival so he could get acquainted with the cold-case case. This action was followed by an email informing Holder that Julio Olivares (aka Loco) was a person of interest in three murders and not just the Rivas murder investigation in Texas.

After coffee and a breakfast of bacon and eggs, the out-of-state Sandoval and the Arizona agent staked out a modest residence on the outskirts of Yuma. Holder informed Sandoval that Loco was a caretaker of the many RV's owned by "Snowbirds" (Canadians), at Araby Acres RV Resort. According to further information received, he was a jack of all trades—a landscape gardener, carpenter, a general fixer-upper, and was kept on at the resort as a security guard after the tourists returned home in spring.

Seated in an unmarked vehicle, the men manned surveillance for some hours outside the home of their suspect.

As evening approached, a green sedan pulled alongside their car. The creepy-looking driver gave the detectives a look from Hell before pulling into the driveway of his home.

"Damn it!" Holder exclaimed. "We've been busted. I'll drive back to the station and assign a stealth team to replace us."

Around four o'clock the next morning, when all was quiet, their replacements did a "dumpster dive," to locate the block plastic bag Loco had tossed in it, for the morning collection. The garbage contents made their way to the Yuma crime lab.

The lab conducted forensic serology tests on certain items retrieved from the garbage—a disposable coffee cup, plastic razor, and some cigarette butts. The lab ultimately concluded that the human saliva and blood from the shaving blade placed Loco at *both* crime scenes, but not at the murder scene of Estrella's daughter.

⚬⟋⟍⚬

On January 2, 2020, in the light of a new dawn, a SWAT team secured the area and blocked off surrounding streets to the Yuma residence. "Come out and let me see your hands," ordered an officer. In the background, a woman's voice pleaded, "No, Mario, please put down the weapon. Whatever you've done, I'll stand by you no matter what. Please, they are going to kill you if you don't do as they say! Please," she begged, "think of our unborn child."

Outside the residence, the game was afoot!

After a forty-five-minute standoff, Loco alias Mario finally surrendered. He slowly exited the property with his hands on his head.

Holder sent a text message to Sandoval back in Texas. "We got the bastard!"

An ecstatic Sandoval replied, "Thank God for that. I'll let the Rivas family know."

Cesar Rivas answered his cellphone. "It's been a long time since we last met."

"I know it has taken twenty-five years," Det. Sandoval relayed, "but we got the bastard that killed your father!"

There was a stunned silence at the other end of the line. Cesar finally found his elated voice, "I will let my mother and my brothers know. Thank you, Carlos, for all you've done for my family. We finally have closure."

Sandoval felt the sting of tears. "I'm happy to have been of assistance. I never break my promises. Now I'm going to enjoy my retirement, go fishing and hunting."

⚬⟊⚬

In the rear of a police vehicle, the handcuffed Loco was read his Miranda Rights but fervently maintained his innocence. "I know nothing about these murders. I wasn't even in the U.S. when they happened. You *pendecos* (dumb assess) have got the wrong man…." In his next breath, he stated, "I'm innocent."

"You are going to need one!" the arresting officer returned. The investigators didn't buy Loco's innocence. They knew better.

⚬⟊⚬

Loco was formally charged with first-degree murder.

The monster remained in the county lockup awaiting extradition to Texas for trial.

Loco would have gotten away with Arnoldo's and Estrella's murders if not for the trace evidence extracted from a beer bottle, fingerprints taken from the refrigerator, his blood on a machete that killed Arnoldo, plus the evidence collected from Estrella's murder.

The Rivas evidence in Cold Case storage since 1994, finally

brought closure for the families of the victims of Loco's madness. And the semen and pubic hairs collected at Estrella's autopsy placed Loco in Laredo, Mexico. However, Aminta's death would be circumstantial, with no direct evidence to put the gang member at the farmhouse. The rock that had bashed in her skull remained unfound.

⚮

The judge denied Julio Luis Olivares, aka Loco, or Mario, bail. Six months later, his trial began in Houston, Texas.

Loco's defense lawyer couldn't argue against the overwhelming evidence: DNA found inside Estrella, or his fingerprint discovered on the tip of a hunting knife embedded in Estrella's head. Nor how both his client's and Arnoldo Riva's blood was present on the machete.

"DNA doesn't lie," the prosecuting attorney stated at the trial. "Your client is guilty of murder!" Case closed, as far as he was concerned.

After an hour of deliberation by the seven women and five men of the jury, Loco was found guilty on two counts of first-degree murder.

For the lead prosecutor, it was a landmark case of indisputable DNA.

Judge Fernando Rodriguez addressed the defendant. "Arnoldo Rivas and Estrella Lozano had everything to live for, and in an instant, you took their lives away. In all probability, you have taken many other lives, including that of a disabled young woman."

At a later hearing, Loco was sentenced to death, to be executed by lethal injection.

"Damn, this shit is for real!" Loco uttered after his death row cell door clanged shut.

While awaiting death, the paranoid schizophrenic inmate claimed he was being spied upon by shadowy grey figures with glowing red orbs. He also stated that he heard the ghostly beings speak in a strange native language. "I'm telling you, they are going to kill me!" Loco bewailed to the correctional officer. "It's like having a bad dream when you are awake!"

The smirking guard laughed, "Well, your *ghosts* will be doing us a big favor. There will be one less lunatic inmate to feed and take care of."

And ethereal karma did just that!

The next morning the same correctional officer made a startling discovery when Loco's cell door was unlocked. Inmate 50290 was stone dead in his cell. He had died right under the noses of the guards! His demise read like a gothic mystery—there was no rational explanation for the circular wound to his heart.

The coroner was dumbfounded. "I have never seen anything like this. It is baffling because the prisoner died from a blow-dart to his chest. His blood sample contained the deadly poison curare. It was inconceivable that he could have possessed such a weapon."

Did a witch's wrath lead to the demise of this merciless killer's life on Earth? Would there now be a peaceful, vindicated astral life for Arnoldo Rivas, Estrella, and Aminta? Were their wanderings as ethereal beings on Earth now over? Or would their ancient roots continue?

Epilogue

Captain Travasso eventually retired from the Ecuadoran police force. He never forgot the American missionary, Belicia Godwin, whom he had "targeted" as a murderer, and confident of his judgment. On his deathbed, some years later, he begged for her forgiveness.

The Pichincha Women's Prison burned to the ground in 1982. The Warden, and the guards who had mistreated Belicia, perished from smoke inhalation, including hundreds of trapped inmates.

Arson was strongly suspected.

The nun who had helped to remove Kayapa's baby and hand her to Belicia vanished into thin air. Many believed that she was a benevolent spirit.

❦

An American cousin of missionary Josiah Godwin fought the Ecuadoran officials for years, to have the remains of their slain family members returned to the U.S. for proper Christian burial.

Finally, in 2018, their skeletal remains were disinterred and shipped to the U.S., where their remains were placed in caskets and buried alongside Josiah Godwin's father and mother.

❦

Antonio Medena, Belicia Godwin's father, eventually retired from his political career, married his secretary, an American mistress of many years, and relocated with her to Florida. Antonio's eventual death, following the toxicology findings, was indeed mysterious. Curare was found in large quantities. Before his demise, Antonio's wife had told her friends that her husband was a deeply "troubled" man. He had never forgiven himself for being absent during his daughter, Belicia's adolescent, teenage, and adult years. But what had sunk him into a deep depression was the knowledge that he had failed to keep his promise to Belicia, by handing over Analena, the Amazonian child that his daughter worshipped, to an orphanage. And that he had never once checked on the welfare of this child.

❦

Sister Mariá, Analena's nemesis, was consigned to a Carmelite Convent, never to utter another word. The orphanage was closed down in 2010 after a health inspector discovered the infestation of rats in the children's dormitories.

oˈɔ

The El Salvadoran military eventually assassinated Dalia and other FMLN rebels. The abortionist, Lourdes, was imprisoned on the orders of the Catholic Church. She died at age ninety-eight.

oˈɔ

Bastien Olivares died at age ninety-two. He, too, never forgot the little person and spoke about her often before he passed away.

Anna Olivares died in a mental institution, totally insane and alone. Her children and family members never visited her. Loco did not learn of her death until he was on death row.

oˈɔ

The former "rogue" priest Hernández who had touched Estrella's life, died peacefully in his sleep. But not all of the holy men got off Scot-free!

oˈɔ

Just as Estrella had foretold, Charro Morales was hunted down and murdered by a rival cartel. His mistress and their two sons died with him. His wife did not share their fate. She died of old age.

Felix Pena was gunned down outside his home, and Miguel Valles fled to Columbia, never seen again.

◌╫◌

Gabor's remains were discovered after the Padilla ranch was sold in 2010. That crime remains unsolved to this day.

◌╫◌

Border agents Dwayne Dalton and Cesar Rivas finally retired and were witnesses at Loco's trial for the murder of Estrella Lozano.

Norma Rivas took her own life on the day Loco received the death sentence. She left a note on the bedside table. It read: *I'm free now to join my beloved husband. Please be happy for me and take care of yourselves until we meet up in Heaven.*

◌╫◌

Detective Sandoval, the crusader for justice, lived a peaceful life, hunting and fishing at his remote cabin in the mountains until diagnosed with Alzheimer's. He spent his remaining days in a care home.

☙

Loco's wife turned her back on her husband and named their daughter Estrella. She relocated to Mexico, married a policeman, and had four more children. She never forgot those horrific images of Estrella and Aminta shown in the courtroom.

☙

Estrella had lost everything. Every family member of her bloodline had perished in the El Salvadoran civil war. The bloodline of Amazonian roots died with Estrella in 2019.

Her foster brothers were never seen again and presumed to be among the dead found in mass graves after the war.

Thankfully, Estrella didn't live long enough to see "Trump's Border Wall" cut though her farmhouse backyard. The property was taken over by squatters who remain there to this day.

☙

Shortly after the coroner released Estrella's then unidentified body, "Jane Doe" was buried in Calvary Catholic Cemetery in Laredo. It was a very emotional day for her three mourners: Agents Dalton and Rivas and Dr. Morgana Saeger.

The quiet environs of the cemetery were to be her final resting place for now.

There was no one left to come to her grave each day, to say how they loved and missed her. But when her identity became known a year later, her remains were exhumed, paid for by the most unlikely of persons—Caitlin Padilla. The Chicago resident had followed the televised court trial of Loco Olivares, and from shown crime scene photographs *knew* who the little person was. Caitlin immediately contacted the Yuma authorities, who then contacted Det. Sandoval in Texas.

He was staggered by Caitlin's knowledge about Estrella and her daughter, personal details she should not have known. Detective Sandoval recalled the informer's statement, "It sickened me to my stomach," Santiago, the snitch, had said.

Detective Sandoval contacted the Mexican authorities. His call was directed to an English-speaking detective, who disclosed the shocking details of Aminta's unsolved murder. He was shocked to learn that Aminta's mother died on the same day by Loco Olivares and several of his gang members. Although Loco was well-known to both the Mexican police and El Salvadoran law-enforcement, he had not been a suspect at the time of Aminta's or Estrella's death.

Before their lengthy conversation ended, the Mexican detective disclosed a macabre fact.

"Aminta Lozano's unclaimed body was shipped to the National Institute of Medical Science in Mexico City. As far as I'm aware, there isn't much left of her body."

Detective Sandoval wanted to throw up.

၄၂၀

Caitlin Padilla paid for the airfare shipping of Estrella's human remains from Texas, a service van at San Salvador Airport to collect her, two 20-gauge metal caskets, and a tombstone.

With Det. Juan Sandoval's direction, the Laredo County provided Estrella's death certificate, and the Medical Science hospital provided Aminta's.

The burial of the little mother and her daughter, "sleeping" together forever in El Salvador, was conducted by a private funeral home. Neither Caitlin nor Det. Sandoval attended the service, but Caitlin had these endearing words carved on the granite gravestone: "In loving memory of two remarkable women, Estrella and Aminta, whose names will be etched in my heart forever."

Not long after Caitlin's generous gestures to bring mother and daughter together, she was diagnosed with rare spinal cancer. She died peacefully in the hospital.

Her ex-husband had predeceased her. DeLeon Padilla was killed in a drive-by shooting shortly after Caitlin had fled back to the United States.

ojo

Cesar Rivas wrote a book about his father's and Estrella's and Aminta's tragic demise. Later, he said in a television interview, "Writing this book has exorcised the nightmares that I endured for many, many years."

Rivas and Dalton remain friends to this day. They have never forgotten the day Estrella washed ashore on their watch. Nor have those whose lives the Little Breadwinner touched before and after her death.

⚜

In February 2020, on the evening of the murder victims' re-burial, all was serene at Ahuachapán cemetery. A westering sun, sinking toward the horizon, cast its departing rays through the overhead sky. Sunset was a glorious tapestry of color: ancient gold, cinnabar, crimson, and a hint of indigo, as twilight approached. A single golden-red ray of pure light cradled the gravestone of mother and child.

After mortal lives of suffering, entwined souls gained their final resting place in the Afterlife.

The End

Afterword

Justice Delayed:
Due to the Legislative Assembly decreeing an amnesty after Peace Accords, there have been many delays in obtaining justice. The heinous crimes committed by the death squads and FMLN during the war have simply faded into history.

Justice Denied:
On November 6 in 2000, former Defense Minister Jose Guillermo Garcia and former National Guard chief Carlos Eugenio Vides Casanova were exonerated, cleared of responsibility to the deaths of the four American churchwomen who were raped and killed by soldiers in 1980. Tried in the U.S., a federal judge said there was not enough evidence linking the retired generals to the murders.

A Note from the Author

"The blisters with moral fury," is the quintessential example of unspeakable acts depicted in the Academy Awarded movie *"Salvador"* directed by Oliver Stone, in which James Woods, Jim Belushi, Michael Murphy, and John Savage bring the shocking truth of this dirty war to light. Or Google: *"El Salvador's Civil War"* as seen through the eyes of American journalist Richard Boyle.

Postscript

REPORT OF THE UNTRUTH COMMISSION ON EL SALVADOR

From Madness to Hope: the 12-Year War in El Salvador

Report of the Commission on the Truth for El Salvador

The Commission on the Truth for El Salvador

Belisario Betancur
CHAIRMAN

Reinaldo Figueredo Planchart
THOMAS BUERGENTHAL

CONTENTS

I. Introduction

II. The Mandate

  A. The mandate

  B. Applicable law

  C. Methodology

III. Chronology of the Violence

IV. Cases and Patterns of Violence

  A. A general overview of causes and patterns of violence

  B. Violence against opponents by agents of the State

    1. Illustrative example: the murders of the Jesuit Priests (1989)

    2. Extrajudicial Executions

      (a) San Francisco Guajoyo (1980)

      (b) The leaders of the Frente Democratico Revolucionario (1980)

      (c) The American churchwomen (1980)

      (d) El Junquillo (1981)

      (e) The Dutch journalists (1982)

      (f) Las Hojas (1983)

      (g) San Sebastían (1988)

      (h) Attack on an FMLN Hospital and execution of a nurse (1989)

      (i) Garcia Arandigoyen (1990)

      (j) Fenastras and Comadres (1989)

      (k) Oquelí and Flores (1990)

ADDITIONAL NOTES

- "US role in Salvador's brutal war."
  —BBC NEWS

- Salvadoran Far-Right Leader ill with cancer.
  —THE NEW YORK TIMES

- Democracy among the Ruins: Citizens struggle with a turbulent campaign.
  —TIME MAGAZINE

- "El Salvador, 11.481a: Irregularities in the investigation."
  —EL SALVADOR 11.481A

- An interview with Edward S. Herman: "Freedom is not on the march."
  —INTERNATIONAL SOCIALIST REVIEW

- *Timeline:* El Salvador: A chronology of key events.
  —BBC NEWS

- "Trial of Salvadoran generals opens in Floris."
  —NATIONAL CATHOLIC REPORTER

- D'Aubuisson Honored by Conservatives at Capitol Hill Dinner.
  —THE WASHINGTON POST

About the Author

Lucia Mann, humanitarian and anti-slavery activist, was born in British colonial South Africa in the wake of World War II. She now resides in British Columbia, Canada. After retiring from freelance journalism in the 1990s, she wrote a four-book African series to give voice to those who have suffered and are suffering brutalities and captivity.

Photo Credit
Deb Booth

BOOKS IN LUCIA MANN'S AFRICAN SERIES
(In sequential order)

Rented Silence
CBC BOOK AWARD WINNER

The Sicilian Veil of Shame
Africa's Unfinished Symphony
INDIE EXCELLENCE AWARD WINNER

A Veil of Blood Hangs over Africa

ALSO BY LUCIA MANN

Addicted to Hate
> LITERARY TITAN AWARD WINNER, WISHING WELL BOOK
> AWARD WINNER, BOOK EXCELLENCE AWARD WINNER,
> INDEPENDENT PRESS AWARD WINNER, IPPY BOOK AWARD
> WINNER, INDEPENDENT PRESS AWARD WINNER

Endless Incarnation Sorrows
> LITERARY TITAN AWARD WINNER, BOOK EXCELLENCE LITERARY
> AWARD WINNER

Visit www.LuciaMann.com and
www.ReportModernDaySlavery.org
for more information on how you can help
alleviate the scourge of modern-day slavery.

www.ingramcontent.com/pod-product-compliance
Lightning Source LLC
Chambersburg PA
CBHW031826090426
42741CB00005B/145